MAN YOUR GRILL

COOKIN' & GRILLIN' WITH BEER!

By: Bonnie Jesseph

www.WinosHaveFun.com
www.WinosBuddies.com

I

W.I.N.O.S. Standard Abbreviations

tsp.	=	teaspoon	sm.	=	small
T.	=	tablespoon	med.	=	medium
c.	=	cup	lg.	=	large
oz.	=	ounce(s)	pl.	=	pint
lb.	=	pound(s)	ql.	=	quart
sq.	=	square	doz.	=	dozen
ctn.	=	carton or container	bu.	=	bushel
pkg.	=	package(s)	env.	=	envelope(s)
btl.	=	bottle(s)	pkl.	=	packet(s)
liter	=	liter	mg.	=	milligram(s)
approx.	=	approximately	gm.	=	gram(s)
temp.	=	temperature	gal.	=	gallon(s)

OTHER W.I.N.O.S. PRODUCTIONS

COOKBOOKS

W.I.N.O.S.™ COOK WITH WINE

W.I.N.O.S. ™ HORMONAL MOMENTS (Cooking with Wine and Chocolate)

W.I.N.O.S. ™ GO TAPAS, Appe-teasers and Mini Meals

W.I.N.O.S. ™ (Women In Need of Spirits)

GLOVIE™ WINE GLASS INSULATORS

COCKTAIL NAPKINS   APRONS   HATS   T-SHIRTS

BOTTLE BRACELETS   MAGNETS   GREETING CARDS   STATIONERY

Cover Design by Sandy Johnson

Thanks to Dee Saltrick for help with the book title.

First Printing - May 2007
Second Printing - December 2007
Third Printing - August 2008
Fourth Printing - April 2010
Fifth Printing - March 2012
Sixth Printing - May 2012

ISBN 978-1-57166-480-8

Making a difference with every sip.®

What is it?

A club for fun loving women (and men) who enjoy food, wine, laughter and getting together for a little "sanity" in their lives, all while giving back and leaving a legacy!

Member Benefits:

Your membership will include:
- Social events such as winery tours, wine tastings, luncheons, shopping, etc.
- On-line newsletter with recipes and wine pairings
- Advice from wine "experts"
- Ideas for entertaining, dinner menus, cocktail parties, girlfriend night "ins"
- Access to WINOS MOMENTS™ - funny quotes and stories to get you through the day, like "what made you want to drink today"!
- Discounts on products from www.winoshavefun.com
- How to start a local WINOS BUDDIES CLUB™ in your area
- Annual meetings, cruises and much, much, more...

Leaving a legacy:

A percentage of every membership will be donated to various worthy causes through your local chapter and on a national level.

SEE OUR WEBSITE FOR MORE DETAILS! www.winoshavefun.com
www.winosbuddies.com

DEDICATION

This book is in memory of my Dad. He was a devoted husband, father and WWII Veteran who had a heart the size of the state of Texas. He loved his country so much he proudly displayed the American Flag on a huge flag pole that was almost bigger than his house. He loved his family more than life, a good football game, his train set, a funny joke, crossword puzzles, great food, his grill and a cold beer. We all miss you, Dad!

This book is also in honor of my big brother, Scott, who is the best brother any sister could ever want. As a Vietnam veteran, "Scottie" learned how to cook with beer from one of his platoon leaders who always poured beer over whatever they were cooking, even if the food came out of a can. He has continued the tradition and cooks, marinates and grills with beer for family and friends. He also loves football, NASCAR, fishing, his new wife, his new boat and, of course, drinking beer. Did I mention he likes his new boat?

This book is also dedicated to all the men and women serving in the military today and especially to our fallen soldiers. May GOD BLESS THEM ALL!!!

Love,
Bonnie

Dear Fellow BEER Guzzlers,

Now, I know it is a little odd to get a cookbook on cookin' and grillin' with BEER from a female author, but allow me to explain. First of all, I am of German descent. Enough said! I was raised on football and beer. I think they put it in my formula when I was a baby. I grew up as a tomboy and played powder puff football until my brother taught me how to tackle. Boy was he ever sorry, HA! He also taught me how to play hockey, all about NASCAR and how to drink beer and burp. What are big brothers for, right? Our mother, who was quite proper, was none too pleased. And my real secret is, I've always wanted to be a racecar driver, or at least do drag racing once in my life. There's always hope, and I'm not dead yet!

Just like my previous two books, this one was a group effort. Friends and family sent me their favorite recipes and some were passed down through the ages from my ancestors. Some recipes I made up as I went and some are "eat at your own risk." I tried to remember to point those out to you. One friend sent one known as his special "fluffer nutter" recipe. Now this one doesn't have beer in it, but it takes a six pack to wash it down!

Many friends sent jokes as well, but some I couldn't put in print, partly because they had some really bad words, but also because I didn't get the joke (I'm blond). My kids even offered to include some of their beer drinking games for the book, but I declined after hearing all about them. The little darlings even offered to teach me. I stopped at Beer Pong!

The Beer Belly Jokes and one-liners are for your enjoyment. Do you have ANY idea how hard it is to find CLEAN beer jokes? It's kind of an oxymoron, so I included golf jokes and whatever else I could find to make you laugh. One fine fellow told me about some jokes written on his bathroom wallpaper. I asked if he would share them with me. Bless his heart, he sat on the "john" with his laptop for who knows how long, and e-mailed them to me. Now that is being a good friend!

Instead of donating to Breast Cancer Research like my first two books, I decided to give a percentage of proceeds of this book to the prevention of heart disease, which, unfortunately, affects **W.I.N.O.S.** (Women in Need of Sanity) and beer guzzlers alike. We are just trying to make a difference for everyone along the way.

Have fun. DON'T DRINK AND DRIVE!
Cheers,

Bonnie Jesseph

Notes & Recipes

_____

_____

_____

_____

_____

_____

_____

_____

_____

_____

_____

_____

_____

_____

_____

_____

Table of Contents

BEER BOMBS..1-12

STARTING LINE UP!...13-32

SOUPS, STEWS, SALADS & SIDE DISHES..........................33-66

MARINADES & SAUCES 67-82

FISH 83-98

POULTRY 99-112

BEEF, VEAL, LAMB & GAME.......................................113-170

BREADS..171-182

DESSERTS 183-200

INDEX...201-208

CONVERTING TO METRIC MEASUREMENTS........................209

FAVORITE RECIPES
FROM MY COOKBOOK

Recipe Name	Page Number

Beer Bombs!

FAVORITE RECIPES
FROM MY COOKBOOK

Recipe Name	Page Number

Beer Bombs!
(Either stay home when you drink these or get a DD)

Dogs Bollocks

7 oz. melon vodka ☺   **2 dashes lime juice**
12 oz. lager ☺

Pour in the vodka first and then proceed to pour the beer on top.

The Canadian Gulp

3 oz. amaretto almond liqueur ☺   **2 oz. Coca-Cola**
1 pt. beer ☺

Pour the amaretto into the jar. Follow it up by pouring a chilled beer (Canadian if possible). Then top it off with the Coke.

Ball Hooter

1 part tequila ☺   **1 glass beer** ☺
1 part peppermint schnapps ☺

Fill a shaker with ice. Pour in equal parts liquor. Shake or swirl. Strain into shot glass(es). Serve with a short, cold glass of beer.

Sip and Get Funky

1 oz. gin ☺
3 oz. beer ☺

1/2 oz. grenadine syrup
1/2 oz. 7-Up soda

Mix ingredients and slam it.

Outhouse Slammer

1 oz. Everclear ☺
3 oz. Coca-Cola

3 oz. beer ☺

Pour the beer and Coca-Cola into a pint glass. Fill a shot glass with Everclear and ignite (carefully). Drop the burning shot of Everclear into the beer-Coke mixture and chug.

The Extinguisher

1/2 oz. vodka ☺
1/2 oz. gin ☺
1/2 oz. rum ☺
1/2 oz. Grand Marnier orange
   liqueur ☺

1/4 oz. Tia Maria coffee
   liqueur ☺
1/4 oz. Kahlua coffee liqueur ☺
1 oz. sweet & sour mix
1 splash cranberry juice
Top with draft beer ☺

Combine all alcohol in a 12-ounce glass with ice. Add sour mix. Add a splash of cranberry juice to form a layer of red at the top of the glass. Top with foam from draft beer tap.

Michelada

12 oz. beer ☺
Juice of 1 lemon
2 dashes Worcestershire sauce
1 dash soy sauce

1 dash Tabasco sauce
1 pinch black pepper
Salt

   Mix ingredients in a tall high glass with lots of ice. Add beer, mix and serve.

Vermo

3 parts Harp lager ☺   **1 part spiced rum** ☺

   Pour into a beer pilsner, and serve.

Good 'n Plenty

1 oz. spiced rum ☺
1 oz. sambuca ☺
1 oz. brandy ☺

1 oz. vodka ☺
1 oz. lemon juice
2 oz. orange juice

   Pour rum, sambuca, brandy, vodka and lemon juice into a cocktail shaker over ice. Add orange juice, shake and strain into an old-fashioned glass. Tastes just like the candy.

Green Goblin

1/2 pt. hard cider
1/2 pt. lager ☺

1 shot Blue Curacao liqueur ☺

Cider first, lager, then Curacao.

Hot 'n' Frosty

1 oz. cinnamon schnapps ☺   **10 oz. frosted glass beer** ☺

Fill a shot glass with cinnamon schnapps. Drop the full shot glass into a frosted mug o' beer, and serve.

Naval Destroyer

1 can frozen limeade concentrate   **3 cans MGD lite lager** ☺
1 can Bacardi white rum ☺

Thaw limeade concentrate and put in pitcher. Pour Bacardi rum into the empty limeade can until full, then transfer to pitcher. Add 3 beers to pitcher and serve over ice in glasses.

Lunch Box

3/4 btl. beer ☺   **1 oz. orange juice**
1 shot amaretto almond liqueur ☺

   Fill a glass almost full with beer. Fill the rest with orange juice (careful not to fill it to the top). Then take the shot of amaretto and drop it into the cup with the beer and orange juice.

Miner's Lung

3 shots vodka ☺   **Fill with Guinness stout** ☺

   Place three shots of vodka into a pint-size beer glass and fill with Guinness stout.

Red Eye

3/4 glass beer ☺   **Tomato juice**
1 oz. vodka ☺

   Pour vodka into a beer glass one half to three-quarters filled with beer. Top with tomato juice and serve.

Faith, Hope and Garrity

1 oz. Irish whiskey ☺
4 oz. V8 vegetable juice
1 tsp. smoky barbecue sauce

1 tsp. lemon juice
6 1/2 oz. beer ☺

Pour the Irish whiskey, V8 juice, barbecue sauce and lemon juice into a highball glass and stir. Fill with beer and serve.

Boilermaker

2 oz. whiskey ☺

10 oz. beer ☺

Fill shot glass with whiskey. Drop full shot glass into mug o' beer. Drink immediately. Enjoy.

Life is a waste of time, time is a waste of life,
so get wasted all of the time and have the time of your life.
--Anonymous

Deer Hunter

The Deer Hunter is a sweet drink, so it's good to use a spicy root beer like Barqs. Invented by Steven Spencer, Will Robinette and Anthony Dedousis in New York City, this drink was originally mixed south of Canal Street near Chinatown and Nancy's Whiskey Pub, a famous dive bar nearby. Nowadays the Deer Hunter is a beverage enjoyed all over the city, particularly with Jagermeister and film afficionados. Be careful, it goes down easy.

2 oz. chilled Jagermeister herbal liqueur ☺
1 oz. vodka ☺

1 squeeze lemon
3 to 5 oz. chilled root beer

Add ice to a Collins glass. Pour Jagermeister and vodka over the ice (Jagermeister should be chilled, of course). Add root beer to fill glass to taste and then finish it off with a squeeze of a lemon-quarter and serve.

Spudgun

4 parts Drambuie Scotch whiskey ☺

2 parts vodka ☺
2 parts beer ☺

Mix it together and hurl it down.

Power Drill

1 part vodka ☺
1 part orange juice

1 splash beer ☺

Almost fill a shot glass with equal parts of orange juice and vodka. Add a splash of beer and serve.

Brian's Juice

12 oz. beer ☺
1 oz. Bacardi limon rum ☺

3 oz. spicy clamato juice

Add the beer and rum to a pint glass. Fill with spicy clamato juice. Sprinkle clamato rimmer on top and serve.

Black and Tan

1 part Bass pale ale ☺

1 part Guinness stout ☺

Fill stein half full with Bass. Next pour Guinness over a spoon slowly until glass is full. If done correctly, the Guinness will stay on top and the Bass on bottom, hence the name Black and Tan.

Heavy Navel

1 oz. vodka ☺
1 oz. peach schnapps ☺

1 oz. Bud Light lager ☺

Pour the vodka and peach schnapps into a cocktail glass and stir. Top with beer and serve.

Flaming Dr. Pepper

**3/4 shot amaretto almond
  liqueur** ☺

1/4 oz. 151 proof rum ☺
1/2 glass beer ☺

Fill a shot glass about 3/4 full with amaretto and top it off with enough 151 proof rum to be able to burn. Place the shot glass in another glass and fill the outer glass with beer (right up to the level of the shot glass). Ignite the amaretto/151 and let it burn for a while. Blow it out (or leave it burning if you're brave - not recommended) and slam it. Tastes just like Dr. Pepper.

Backfire on the Freeway

2 oz. Bacardi 151 rum ☺

6 oz. Guinness stout ☺

Drop a double shot of 151 into a beer mug of Guinness and chug immediately.

Baha Fog

1 can beer ☺   **1/4 lime**
Tequila ☺

Open a Corona and fill it to the top with tequila. Squeeze a 1/4 lime on top. Chug immediately.

Bite Me

1 oz. rum ☺   **1 oz. orange soda**
1 oz. A&W root beer

Pour the rum, root beer and soda into a cocktail shaker half-filled with ice cubes. Shake well and strain into a cocktail glass. Garnish with orange peel and serve.

Beeraquirilla

5 oz. Bud Light lager ☺   **1/2 oz. light rum** ☺
1 handful ice   **3 oz. strawberry daiquiri mix**
1/2 oz. tequila ☺   **3 oz. margarita mix**

Pour into a blender in this order: ice, beer, tequila, rum, daiquiri mix, margarita mix. Blend until frothy, then pour.

AJ's Bubbling Brew

1 oz. 151 proof rum ☺
1 oz. tequila ☺
1 oz. Southern Comfort peach
   liqueur ☺

1 oz. peppermint schnapps ☺
12 oz. beer ☺

Carefully pour the rum, tequila, Southern Comfort and peppermint schnapps into the glass. Light on fire and quickly add the beer. After adding the beer, stir the mixture and watch it bubble forth.

Celtic War Party

This drink finds its origins in British Columbia, Canada. The contributor (Dan) invented this recipe by tinkering with his own tastes slowly, trying to find something with a strong complex flavor. Warning: this drink will sneak up on you fast.

1 oz. Jagermeister herbal
   liqueur ☺
1 oz. Crown Royal Canadian
   whiskey ☺

1/2 oz. Goldschlager cinnamon
   schnapps ☺
1 pt. Guinness stout ☺

Add all ingredients to a cocktail shaker half-filled with ice cubes. Shake well, strain into a pint glass and serve.

Bud Bomb Breakfast

12 oz. ice cold Budweiser lager ☺   **2 oz. V8 vegetable juice**

  Fill a chilled beer mug about 3/4 full with lager. Top off with the V8 spicy vegetable juice and serve.

Beer Buster

2 oz. 100 proof Smirnoff vodka ☺   **2 dashes Tabasco sauce**
8 oz. chilled beer ☺

  Pour Smirnoff vodka into a highball glass and fill with beer or ale. Add dashes of Tabasco sauce, stir lightly and serve.

WARNING: The consumption of alcohol may cause you to think you can sing.
--Anonymous

Starting Line Up!
(Appetizers)

FAVORITE RECIPES
FROM MY COOKBOOK

Recipe Name	Page Number

Starting Line Up!
(Appetizers)

Caramelized Garlic Breath

29 cloves garlic, whole & peeled
1 btl. beer ☺
1 T. butter

2 T. vegetable broth
2 tsp. brown sugar

Preheat oven to 350°. In a medium saucepan over medium heat, bring garlic and beer to a boil. Simmer, covered, until the garlic is tender, about 10 to 12 minutes. Remove and drain. In an 8- or 9-inch baking dish, arrange garlic in a single layer.

Meanwhile, cook sugar in a medium skillet over medium heat, stirring often. The sugar will melt and start to thicken. Add butter and broth and bring to a boil. Pour sauce over garlic cloves. Bake 15 to 25 minutes, or until the sauce is thick. Remove from oven; cover with foil and allow to stand for 5 minutes.

Serve warm or at room temperature with crusty French bread or toast corners.

Scientists say that 2 beers a day will make you live longer.
So just think what beer jokes can do for you.
--Anonymous

Chilly Cheese Dip

2 T. salad oil
1/4 sm. onion, minced
12 oz. Cheddar cheese, cut into
  1/2" chunks
1 (4 oz.) can chopped green chili,
  drained & peeled

1/4 to 1/3 c. beer ☺
1/4 tsp. salt (opt.)
1/8 tsp. hot pepper sauce (Tabasco)
1 sm. tomato, chopped
1/8 tsp. ground cumin

In a 2-quart saucepan over medium heat, cook onion until tender. Add all other ingredients, except the tomato. Cook over medium heat until the cheese is melted and mixture is smooth. Stir in tomato.
  Serve with chips.

My wife and I had words,
But I didn't get to use mine.

--Anonymous

Cheezy-Weezy Beer Dip

This is great with corn chips, rye or pumpernickel bread. You can also use those little party loaves.

2 lb. sharp Cheddar cheese, room
  temp.
2 cloves garlic
3 T. Worcestershire sauce, or more,
  to taste

1 tsp. dry mustard
Tabasco sauce, to taste
1/2 btl. beer (dark, if possible) ☺
1 tsp. salt

Cut the cheese into cubes and place them in a food processor or electric mixer. Process until perfectly smooth. Add the garlic, Worcestershire sauce, mustard and Tabasco sauce. Blend well. Add the beer, a little at a time, while continuing to beat the cheese, until the mixture is a good, firm spreading consistency. Too much beer will make the cheese too fluffy. Stir in the salt and refrigerate.
  Will keep in refrigerator for a week.

I was married by a judge. I should have asked for a jury.
--Groucho Marx

"Bubba's" Beer Batter

(Onion Rings, Tomatoes, Zucchini or Shrimp)

This is a great batter to fry up whatever you have in your vegetable bin.

1 beer ☺
1 T. baking powder
1 egg, beaten
1 1/2 c. flour

Vegetable oil, for deep-frying
1 lg. onion, sliced thin (sweet
   onions are my favorite)
Salt, to taste

Combine beer, baking powder and egg in a large bowl. Stir flour into mixture. Heat oil. Separate onion into rings; dip rings in batter to coat. Fry a few rings at a time in the oil, until golden brown. Remove and drain on paper towels.
   Enjoy.

By all means, marry. If you get a good wife, you'll become happy;
if you get a bad one, you'll become a philosopher.
--Socrates

Con Queso Dip

1 c. grated Cheddar cheese
1 c. grated Monterey Jack cheese
1 c. Gorgonzola cheese
1 c. Colby cheese
1 btl. beer (your choice but not
   dark beer) ☺

1 sm. or med. onion, minced
1 T. unsalted butter
2/3 c. tomatoes, chopped
Chopped jalapeño peppers, to
   taste
Tortilla Chips

In a bowl, toss the cheeses with the flour and reserve the mixture. In a large heavy saucepan, cook the onion with the butter over low heat, stirring, until it is softened and clear (do not burn). Add the beer, the tomatoes and the peppers (jalapeño) and simmer the mixture for 5 minutes. Add the reserved cheese mixture by 1/2 cupfuls to the beer mixture, stirring after each addition until the cheeses are melted. Serve the dip with the chips.

Beer-Boiled Shrimp

2 c. beer, your choice ☺
2 sm. onions, sliced
1 garlic clove
1 to 2 bay leaves
3 whole peppercorns

3 celery stalks
2 tsp. salt
1/2 lime or lemon, quartered
2 lb. lg. shrimp, cleaned

In a large pot, bring to a boil. Add all ingredients, except lime (or lemon). Simmer until they turn pink. Add lemon. Remove from heat, drain and cool. Peel shells and chill.

Beer-Battered Veggies

1 1/2 c. beer ☺
2 c. white flour
2 eggs
1 c. whole milk
Salt & pepper
2 c. canola or safflower oil

1 carrot, cut into thick strips
1 onion, sliced into rings
1 green bell pepper, sliced in rings
1 sm. zucchini, sliced in thin discs
12 fresh button mushrooms

Mix 1 1/2 cups flour with the beer and let stand for at least 3 hours at room temperature. Mix eggs and milk, then in a separate bowl, mix together 1/2 cup flour and salt and pepper to taste. Heat oil to 375° in a deep skillet or frying pot. Dip each vegetable in the egg and milk mixture, fully covering each piece. Dip the vegetable into the flour and seasoning mixture, then dip the vegetable into the beer and flour mixture. Carefully place the vegetables into the oil. Fry until golden brown.

Dip into ranch, blue cheese or horseradish dressing or your favorite dressing.

"bread, meat, green vegetables and zythos (beer)",
--Greek writer Sophocles' (450 BC) suggested diet

Welsch Rabbit with Beer

(AKA - Beer Cheese)

1 T. butter	1/2 tsp. salt
1 lb. sharp Cheddar cheese, grated	1/2 tsp. Worcestershire sauce
3/4 c. beer ☺	1 egg, slightly beaten
Dash of Tabasco sauce	Tomato slices
1 tsp. dry mustard	Toast

Melt butter in top of double boiler. Add beer (minus 1 tablespoon) and cheese. Mix seasonings with 1 tablespoon beer and add to cheese. Stir in egg. Serve over toast and tomato slices.

Serve with vegetables and olives.

My wife has a slight impediment in her speech.
Every now and then she stops to breathe.
--Jimmy Durante

Fried Zucchini in Beer Batter

1 med. zucchini, thinly sliced
2 tsp. salt
1/4 tsp. pepper
1 c. flour
1 1/2 tsp. baking powder

1/2 tsp. baking soda
1/2 c. beer (Drink the rest!)☺
1/4 c. fresh lemon juice
1 c. vegetable oil

Arrange zucchini on piece of waxed paper; salt and pepper both sides, using 1 teaspoon of salt and pepper. Combine flour, baking powder, baking soda and remaining teaspoon salt in medium-size bowl. Remove 1/2 cup of the mixture to a piece of waxed paper. Dip both sides of zucchini in the 1/2 cup flour mixture.

Stir beer and lemon juice into remaining flour mixture. (Mixture will foam.) Stir until consistency of pancake batter. Heat oil in large skillet. Dip zucchini into batter and sauté half at a time in hot oil, about 3 minutes on each side. Keep warm in oven while sautéing remaining zucchini. Serve immediately.

A long time ago, way back in history
When all there was to drink was nothing but cups of tea,
Along came a man by the name of Charlie Mopps
And he invented a wonderful drink and he made it out of hopps...
--Drinking song

Wing 'a Ding 'n Drummies

8 to 10 servings

Make ahead 1 day or start in morning. Very good!

1 c. soy sauce
1 c. pineapple juice
1 clove garlic, pressed
2 T. minced onion
1 tsp. ground ginger
1/4 c. brown sugar

1 (7 oz.) can beer ☺
1/4 c. butter or oil
2 pkg. drumettes chicken wings,
the part that looks like little
drumsticks

Combine first 8 ingredients and stir until dissolved. Pour over chicken and marinate overnight, or at least 8 hours. Be sure to cover all pieces. Drain and save marinade.

In a large skillet, pour a small amount of oil and brown chicken on all sides over medium heat. When brown, add 1/2 cup marinade; cover, reduce heat and simmer 15 to 20 minutes. Stir and add more marinade, if necessary. This may be cooked a day ahead and then reheated in oven before serving. Add marinade to moisten before heating. Serve hot on chafing dish.

The problem with the world is that everyone is a few drinks behind.
--Humphrey Bogart

Cheese n' Beer Fondue

This is great with homemade beer bread or just buy a loaf of wheat, white or sourdough bread - not sliced. Cut bread into cubes for dunking. Yummy.

4 T. butter
1/4 c. all-purpose flour
1 btl. lager beer ☺
1/2 tsp. Worcestershire sauce

1/4 tsp. dry mustard
1/4 tsp. cayenne pepper, or more,
   to taste
4 c. shredded Cheddar cheese

Melt butter in a medium saucepan over medium heat. Whisk in flour and cook for 1 to 2 minutes, while stirring constantly, to make a roux (a white creamy sauce). Add beer and bring to slow boil. Reduce heat and simmer, stirring occasionally, until mixture thickens to the consistency of heavy cream. Add Worcestershire sauce, mustard and cayenne, stirring thoroughly. Add cheese, one cup at a time, melting cheese after each addition. Stir fondue until it is smooth.
Put in fondue pot or small crock-pot and put out bread and skewers.

Give me a woman who loves beer and I will conquer the world.
--Kaiser Wilhelm

Spicy Fondue

4 servings

Make sure you don't stand downwind from your friends after they've eaten this.

1 can refried or drained black beans
2 c. Cheddar cheese, grated
3 T. minced green onion
1 or 2 cloves garlic, chopped small
1/2 to 1 tsp. Worcestershire sauce (the more the spicier)

1 cayenne pepper, seeded & chopped, or 1 to 2 tsp. dried cayenne
1 chile pepper, seeded & chopped
3/4 to 1 c. beer, room temp. ☺

Combine refried beans or black beans, Cheddar cheese, butter, scallion, garlic, Worcestershire sauce, cayenne pepper and chile pepper in a heavy saucepan.

Heat, stirring, until mixture is heated thoroughly, 10 to 15 minutes. Add beer gradually, while stirring. Transfer to a fondue pot.

Serve with tortilla chips or fresh vegetables for dipping.

The church is near, but the road is icy. The bar is far away, but I will walk carefully.
--Russian proverb

Easy Kielbasa Fondue

1 to 1 1/2 lb. fully-cooked kielbasa (can also use low-fat turkey sausage), cut into 1/2" slices on diagonal

2 c. beer (your choice) ☺

8 to 10 oz. shredded sharp Cheddar cheese

2 c. shredded Swiss cheese

2 T. flour

1/2 tsp. dry mustard

1/4 tsp. pepper, or to taste

1 clove garlic, peeled & cut in half

1/8 tsp. hot sauce (like Tabasco)

Heat sausage and about 1/2 cup beer, and bring to a boil. Reduce heat and simmer, uncovered, for about 10 minutes, and drain. Combine Cheddar cheese, Swiss cheese, mustard, flour and pepper until cheese is coated. Rub bottom and sides of heavy saucepan with garlic clove. Add rest of the beer. Heat until bubbles rise to surface. Add cheese mixture, about one cup at a time, constantly stirring until melted and smooth. Add hot sauce to taste. Put in fondue pot. Serve with sliced kielbasa. If sauce is too thick add more beer to thin it.

The best wood in most amateurs' bags is the pencil.
--Anonymous

Buffalo Wings for a Party

3 doz. chicken wings, wing tips
   removed
2 btl. beer (your choice) ☺
1 c. molasses
1/2 c. creamy peanut butter
1/2 c. fresh lemon juice
1/2 c. Worcestershire sauce

1/3 c. prepared mustard
1 tsp. salt
2 T. chili powder
1/4 c. chopped fresh parsley, for
   garnish
1 to 2 lemons, sliced thin, for
   garnish

Preheat oven to 450°. Line a large roasting pan with foil. Cut chicken wings in half at the joint and place wings evenly in roasting pan.

In a large, heavy saucepan, combine the beer, molasses, peanut butter, lemon juice, Worcestershire sauce, mustard, salt and chili powder. Bring to a boil, reduce heat and simmer over low heat about 15 minutes, until sauce has reduced and thickened. Pour sauce over chicken wings, tossing to coat each wing. Bake for 20 minutes. Remove from the oven and let rest for 10 minutes. Place wings on a large platter, and sprinkle with chopped parsley. Garnish with lemon slices and serve.

If you can't handle spicy foods, reduce the amount of Worcestershire sauce and chili powder; or increase if you like hot and spicy.

Is it me - or do the buffalo wings taste like chicken?
--Anonymous

"Bull Fightin" Black Bean and Beef Chili Dip

You can make this in advance for a weekend get-together. Makes enough for a crowd. I serve with Scoops Tortilla chips or large corn chips for easier dipping.

1 T. olive oil
1 med. onion, chopped
1 med. green bell pepper, cored, seeded & chopped
3 garlic cloves, chopped
1 or 2 jalapeños, seeded & minced
1 1/2 lb. ground sirloin or meat loaf mix
2 T. chili powder, or more, to taste
2 tsp. ground cumin
2 tsp. dried oregano

1 lg. can diced tomatoes in juice
1 (8 oz.) can tomato sauce
1/2 c. lager beer ☺
1 tsp. salt
1/2 tsp. ground black pepper
1 (15 1/2 to 19 oz.) can black or pinto beans, drained & rinsed
1 c. sour cream, for garnish
1 c. shredded extra-sharp Cheddar cheese

Heat oil in a large saucepan over medium heat. Add the onion, bell pepper, garlic and jalapeño, and cook, stirring often, until the onion softens, about 6 minutes. Add the beef and cook, stirring and breaking up the meat with the side of a spoon until the meat loses its pink color, about 10 minutes. Drain off the fat.

Continued on following page.

Continued from preceding page.

Add the chili powder, cumin and oregano, and stir for 30 seconds. Stir in the tomatoes with their juice, the tomato sauce, beer, salt and pepper. Bring to a simmer. Reduce the heat to medium-low and cook until thickened, about 45 minutes. During the last 10 minutes, add the beans. Remove from the heat and let stand for 5 minutes, then skim the fat that has risen to the surface. (The dip can be prepared up to 2 days ahead. Reheat gently over medium-low heat.)

Transfer to a heatproof serving bowl. Spoon the sour cream in the center, sprinkle the cheese around the sour cream, and serve hot accompanied by tortilla chips or corn chips.

Without question, the greatest invention in the history of mankind is beer.
Oh, I grant you that the wheel was also a fine invention,
but the wheel does not go nearly as well with pizza.
--Dave Barry

"Macho Nachos"

10 to 12 servings

1/4 c. lime juice
1/4 c. olive oil
1/3 to 1/2 c. beer ☺
2 or 3 cloves garlic, minced or
   pressed (I always add more)
1 tsp. ground cumin
1 fresh jalapeño chili, stemmed,
   seeded & minced
1 can refried beans
1 lb. beef skirt or flank steak (can
   also use chicken)

2 med. onions, chopped &
   browned
1 c. shredded Cheddar cheese
Guacamole (purchased or
   homemade)
Lime Salsa
Flour tortilla chips or corn tortilla
   chips (you can use store-bought
   or make homemade)

Mix lime juice, oil, beer, garlic, cumin and chili; remove 3 tablespoons marinade and set it aside for the beans. Place steak and marinade in large plastic bag and seal. Rotate bag and set it in a large pan. Chill for at least 2 hours, or up until next day, turning occasionally. Grill meat until brown and cooked to your liking, 3 to 5 minutes per side for rare steak. Thinly slice meat crosswise, then cut each slice in half again.

Combine refried beans and reserved marinade and heat. Spread hot beans into a 10-inch round on a large ovenproof platter. Top evenly with onions and steak; sprinkle with cheese. Broil until cheese melts. Remove from oven and top with guacamole and lime salsa. Tuck tortilla chips around edges.

Continued on following page.

Continued from preceding page.

LIME SALSA:

Makes 2 1/2 cups

1 lg. tomato, cored & finely diced
2 lg. tomatillos, husks removed &
  chopped
1/4 c. minced red bell pepper

3 T. minced red onion
1 tsp. grated lime peel
1 T. lime juice

Mix all ingredients together. Serve, or let stand, covered, up to 2 hours.

FLOUR TORTILLA CHIPS:

Makes 8 cups

8 flour tortillas, cut into 8 wedges
  each

2 T. salad oil

Fill lightly-oiled baking pan with a single layer of wedges; brush tops lightly with oil. Bake in a 500° oven until golden and crisp, 5 to 7 minutes. Repeat until all chips are baked.

If you find you do not mind playing golf in the rain, the snow,
even during a hurricane, here's a valuable tip: your life is in trouble.
--Anonymous

"Buckin" Barbecue Cocktail Sausage

2 pkg. cocktail sausage
2 c. barbecue sauce

1 c. brown sugar
2 cans or btl. beer ☺

Put in slow-cooker for about 2 hours. Can also use container with lid and put in oven over low heat.

Easy Beer, Cheese and Veggie Dip

Fill large pot with water, chopped celery and onion (about 1 1/2 cups each). Cook until tender and drain.

In large pan, mix 4 chicken bouillon cubes with 1 can or bottle of beer ☺. Add 1 pound Velveeta cheese and heat until melted. Add cooked celery and onion. Top with Parmesan cheese or cracker crumbs.

Can also add cooked hot sausage, hamburger or chicken.

Serve with your favorite crackers.

What contemptible scoundrel has stolen the cork to my lunch?
--W.C. Fields

Sissy-Chicken Salad Puffy Shells

Can also use tuna, ham or egg salad to stuff.

1 c. beer (Drink the rest) ☺   **1/2 tsp. salt**
1/2 c. butter   **2 T. Parmesan cheese**
1 tsp. all-purpose flour

In saucepan, bring beer to a boil; reduce heat. Add butter and stir until melted. With a wooden spoon, stir in flour and add salt all at once. Cook, stirring until mixture forms into a ball and leaves side of pan. Remove from heat. Add eggs, one at a time, beating well after every addition until smooth. Stir in cheese, Drop by teaspoonful onto buttered baking sheet, swirling top of each (allow room for expansion). Bake at 450° for 10 minutes, reduce heat to 350° and bake 20 minutes more, or until lightly browned. Cool on racks. Split and fill puffs with your favorite egg, ham, tuna or chicken salad.

WARNING: The consumption of alcohol may actually cause pregnancy.
--Anonymous

"Fluffer Nutter" Sandwich

Great appetizer if you're starved.

6-pack of your favorite beer ☺
3 T. or more marshmallow creme

3 T. or more of your favorite
chunky peanut butter
2 slices bread

Spread marshmallow creme on 1 slice of bread. Spread peanut butter on the other slice. Slap them together. Drink one beer with each bite.

This was sent in from a friend who admits he can't cook but enjoys beer! Try at your own risk.

24 hours in a day, 24 beers in a case. Coincidence?
--Stephen Wright

Soups, Stews,
Salads & Side Dishes

FAVORITE RECIPES
FROM MY COOKBOOK

Recipe Name	Page Number

Soups, Stews, Salads & Side Dishes

Soups & Stews

Beer Stew

3 to 4 lb. boneless chuck, cut into
   1" cubes
1 c. flour
2 tsp. salt
1 tsp. pepper
1/3 c. vegetable shortening
6 lg. onions, peeled & quartered

1 (10 1/2 oz.) can condensed beef
   broth
1/2 tsp. thyme, crumbled
3 cloves garlic, chopped
2 c. beer ☺
1/4 c. parsley, chopped
1 bay leaf

  Mix flour, salt and pepper and roll meat cubes in mixture. Heat shortening in a Dutch oven, brown meat cubes on all sides. Add remaining ingredients. Cover tightly and simmer 1 to 2 hours, or until beef is tender. Stir occasionally and add water as needed to keep stew from sticking.

Belgian Beef Stew

2 lb. stew beef
2 1/2 tsp. salt
1/2 c. salad oil
1 clove garlic, chopped fine
1 T. soy sauce
2 bay leaves
2 lb. potatoes, cut into bite-size
  pieces
1 (10 oz.) box frozen peas

1/4 c. flour
1/2 tsp. pepper
2 lb. onions, peeled & sliced
1 can beer ☺
1 T. Worcestershire sauce
1/2 tsp. dried thyme
6 to 8 carrots, cut into bite-size
  pieces

Combine flour, salt and pepper and coat beef well. In 1/4 cup oil, sauté onion and garlic until tender. Set aside. Heat remaining oil. Add beef and brown well. In large pot, add onion, garlic and remaining ingredients, except the box of frozen peas. Add water to cover ingredients. Bring to boiling, then simmer for 2 hours. Add frozen peas and heat thoroughly before serving.

WARNING: The consumption of alcohol is the leading
cause of inexplicable rug burns on the forehead.
--Anonymous

Beef and Beer Stew

4 servings

2 btl. lager ☺
2 1/4 c. water
1 1/2 to 2 lb. ground beef (or I use a
good quality cut of beef cut into
bite-size cubes)
4 to 6 potatoes
3 celery stalks

1 to 2 onions, chopped
4 to 6 cloves garlic, finely chopped
Fresh pepper, to taste (I use a lot)
Salt
Butter
Chili pepper (opt.)

Brown meat in skillet and drain off fat. In a large pot, sauté onions and garlic in butter. Add the celery, carrots, potatoes, cooked beef, water and stir in pepper. Pour in beer; stir and add salt to taste. Boil for 1 to 2 minutes and simmer for close to an hour. Add pepper as desired. Serve with warm bread and a salad.

Beer is good food.
--Anonymous

Irish Stew

16 oz. warm stout ☺
16 oz. beef stock
2 lb. beef chuck, 1" cubes, 2 T. butter
1 lg. onion, sliced
Salt & pepper, to taste
3 cloves garlic, minced

2 T. flat leaf parsley
3 carrots, 1" slices, chopped
6 red potatoes, 1" cubes (with or without skins)
1 T. flour
1 T. tomato paste
4 T. olive oil

Season beef with salt and pepper and dredge in flour. In heavy bottomed 4-quart pot, heat butter and olive oil until hot, but not smoking. Sauté beef until browned on all sides. Set aside and keep warm. In same pot, sauté garlic and onion until translucent. Add carrots and tomato paste. Sauté for 3 minutes, stirring constantly. Add beef, potatoes, beer and beef stock (this should just cover the ingredients in the pot, so add beer first and then beef stock to cover). Bring to a boil for 3 minutes, reduce heat and simmer covered for approximately 1 hour, or until beef is tender. Add more salt and pepper. Turn off the heat, then stir in parsley.

An Irishman is the only man in the world who will step over the bodies of a dozen naked women to get to a bottle of stout.
--Anonymous

Stewed Beef and Bread

6 servings

2 lb. beef stew meat	1/4 c. tomato paste
2 c. peeled & stewed roma tomatoes	2 btl. beer ☺
	1 qt. beef stock
1 med. red onion	2 oz. olive oil
1 c. carrot, cut into bite-size chunks	1 tsp. fresh rosemary
	1/4 tsp. fresh thyme
1 c. celery, cut into bite-size chunks	Pinch of salt & pepper

Heat oven to 350°. Season the meat with salt and pepper. In a small stockpot, heat oil and sear the seasoned beef until brown. Add the vegetables and tomato paste. Cook until they cool lightly. Add the beer and stock and bring to a boil. Reduce to a simmer and add the herbs. Cover and place in the oven. Cook for 1 hour.

Remove from oven and taste. The meat should be tender and the sauce slightly thickened. Adjust seasoning as necessary. Serve in hollowed-out 6-ounce sourdough bread loaves or French rolls.

I never drink anything stronger than gin before breakfast.
--Anonymous

Easy and Quick Beef Stew

1 1/2 to 2 lb. lean ground beef chuck (or I use leftover roast beef sometimes)
1/4 c. all-purpose flour
3 T. unsalted butter or margarine
2 c. fresh chopped onions (2 med.- lg. yellow onions)
2 lg. garlic cloves, minced
1/2 tsp. dried thyme, crumbled
1/4 tsp. freshly-grated nutmeg

1 1/2 lb. red-skin potatoes, scrubbed & cut into 1 1/2" chunks but not peeled
1 (10 1/2 oz.) can beef consommé
1 (12 oz.) can beer ☺, blended with 3 T. all-purpose flour
1 (9 oz.) pkg. frozen asparagus cuts (do not thaw)
Salt & freshly-ground pepper

Shape ground chuck into large flat patty and dredge both sides well in flour. (If using leftover beef roast, skip this.) Heat butter in medium-size Dutch oven over high heat for 1 minute. Add ground beef patty and brown 3 minutes on each side. Lift to plate and reserve. Lower heat to moderate; heat onions, garlic, thyme and nutmeg to drippings and sauté, stirring often, until onions are golden, about 3 minutes. Add potatoes and consommé; bring to a gentle boil, set lid on crooked and cook 15 minutes. Add beer mixture and cook, stirring often, until liquid thickens slightly, 3 to 5 minutes. Add meat, breaking into largish clumps; cover and cook 10 minutes more. Add asparagus and cook, breaking up frozen clumps, until potatoes are tender and meat shows no signs of pink, 7 to 10 minutes more. Remove thyme sprigs. Season to taste with salt and pepper. Ladle into heated soup plates and serve.

Seafood Chowder

Very good!

2 T. olive oil
5 to 6 cloves garlic, minced
2 bay leaves
1 med. onion, chopped
6 med. red potatoes, cubed
   (about 4 c.)
4 med. carrots, sliced (about 2 c.)

10 c. vegetable stock
1 (12 oz.) btl. beer ☺
1 lb. salmon, cubed (can also use
   other fish, grouper is excellent!)
1 lb. fresh bay scallops
1 lb. cocktail shrimp
1/4 c. fresh dill, chopped

In a large pot over medium heat, simmer vegetables, garlic and bay leaves in olive oil, about 10 to 15 minutes. Add 10 cups vegetable stock and beer, stirring frequently until hot. Add seafood and dill, and cook until the vegetables are tender and the seafood is cooked through. Season to taste and serve with crusty French bread.

Golf can best be defined as an endless series of tragedies obscured by the occasional miracle, followed by a good bottle of beer.
--Anonymous

Broccoli Cheese Soup

1 qt. water
1 sm. onion, chopped
1 box chopped broccoli, or 1 lb.
   fresh
1 oz. beef bouillon base (dry)
1 1/2 sticks butter
1 1/2 c. flour
1/4 tsp. garlic powder
1/4 tsp. white pepper

Seasoning salt, to taste
Cayenne pepper, to taste
2 lb. Cheddar &/or American
   cheese, cubed
1 qt. milk
1/8 can beer ☺ (may need more
   depending on desired
   consistency of soup)

Put butter in pan and add onion and broccoli (can use fresh, pre-cooked); cook until onion is transparent. Slowly add flour. Add seasonings and slowly melt cheese. Add remaining ingredients and season to taste. Serve when hot.

Not all chemicals are bad. Without chemicals such as hydrogen and oxygen, for example, there would be no way to make water, a vital ingredient in beer.
--Dave Barry

Beer and Cheese Soup

1/2 c. butter
1 c. flour
4 c. chicken broth
1 1/2 c. cream
1 (16 oz.) jar Cheez Whiz (can use the spicy variety, too!)

6 oz. beer ☺
1 T. Worcestershire sauce
1/2 tsp. egg yolk or yellow food coloring
1/4 c. chives or onion

In heavy pan, melt butter and gradually add flour until completely blended. Slowly add chicken broth and cream. Mix until smooth and thick. Heat over low flame for 5 minutes, stirring occasionally. Add cheese and mix until all cheese is melted and smooth. Add beer and Lea & Perrins. Mix in color and chives. Simmer for about 15 minutes, stirring constantly.

Warning: The consumption of alcohol may lead you to believe you are invisible.
--Anonymous

Potato Beer Soup

Makes 3 to 4 quarts

3 c. water
1 (12 oz.) can beer ☺
1 c. chopped celery

1 c. chopped carrots
1 c. chopped onion
1 c. chopped ham (opt.)

In large pot of water add:

4 chicken bouillon cubes

2 1/2 c. potatoes, cubed

Cook for 30 minutes.
Add carrots, onions and celery. Cook for 10 to 15 minutes.

2 cans cream of chicken soup or mushroom soup

20 oz. frozen mixed vegetables (opt.)

Add and cook 10 minutes.

Before serving, add:
1 lb. Velveeta cheese, cut in cubes

Melt cheese and serve.

Mushroom and Beer Soup

4 to 6 servings

This recipe calls for 6 beers! If you only have 6 beers to your name, you decide if you want to make soup or drink all 6 and skip dinner all together!

6 T. olive oil	2 eggs
2 c. mushrooms, chopped	4 T. heavy cream
2 lg. onions, chopped	Chopped parsley
6 cans beer ☺	Salt & pepper, to taste
1 bay leaf	Grated Gruyére cheese

Pour the oil into a soup pot. Add the mushrooms and onions. Sauté them lightly for a few minutes over low heat. Add the beer and bay leaf and raise the heat to medium. Bring the soup to a boil, then simmer slowly for about 20 minutes.

In the meantime, in a bowl, beat and blend well the eggs and cream. Add some of the hot soup to the egg mixture and blend thoroughly. Pour the mixture into the soup, mixing well. Add the chopped parsley, salt and pepper; mix well. Reheat the soup over medium heat and continue stirring for a few minutes. Remove the bay leaf and serve the soup hot. Sprinkle some grated cheese on top of each serving.

Sweet Potato Soup

6 servings

This is really good!

1/4 c. dark raisins
1 (12 oz.) btl. light beer (Bud works) ☺
4 T. (1/2 stick) butter
1 onion, diced
2 tart apples, unpeeled, cored & diced
1 T. best-quality curry powder
2 tsp. finely-minced fresh ginger root
2 T. unbleached all-purpose flour
Pam cooking spray
3 to 4 c. any well-flavored chicken or vegetable stock
1/4 c. thawed frozen apple juice concentrate, or more, to taste
1 (1") piece cinnamon stick
1 tsp. soy sauce, or more, to taste
2 med. sweet potatoes, peeled & finely diced
Salt & freshly-ground white pepper, to taste
Cayenne pepper, to taste
1 red-skinned apple, cored & cut into lg. julienne, for garnish
Whipped cream, sour cream or plain yogurt, for garnish
Thin lemon wedges, for serving

In a bowl, soak the raisins in the beer for at least 30 minutes or as long as overnight. When you are ready to start making the soup, melt the butter in a 10-inch skillet over medium heat. Add the onion and sauté until it starts

Continued on following page.

Continued from preceding page.

to soften, about 3 minutes. Add the diced apples and sauté again until somewhat softened, 3 to 4 minutes. Sprinkle with the curry powder, turn down the heat to medium-low and cook, stirring often, about 8 minutes. Stir in the ginger and cook 2 minutes longer.

Meanwhile, drain the raisins, reserving both the beer and the raisins. Sprinkle the flour over the apple mixture and cook over low heat 1 minute. Gradually add the beer, stirring to smooth any lumps and cook until hot, smooth and free of floury taste, 5 to 7 minutes. Transfer this mixture to a food processor or blender. Add the raisins and blend until smooth.

Spray a heavy enameled soup pot with the Pam; add the stock, apple juice concentrate, cinnamon stick and soy sauce. Bring to a boil, add the sweet potatoes and turn down the heat. Simmer, partially-covered, until the potatoes are tender, about 30 minutes. Remove the cinnamon stick from the hot stock and stir in the apple purée. Season with salt and white pepper. You may wish to add a bit more apple juice concentrate to sweeten it, a pinch of cayenne pepper if you want it spicier, and/or a little more soy sauce. Simmer over low heat for several minutes more to meld the flavors.

Ladle the hot soup into bowls, sprinkle each bowl with the julienned apple and top with a spoonful of whipped cream, sour cream or yogurt.

Can add lemon or not. Good both ways.

When You're Broke Beer Soup

2 or 3 servings

This is when you don't have much left in the refrigerator, except beer and eggs.

4 cans beer (total 48 oz.)☺
5 T. sugar
1 tsp. cinnamon
6 egg yolks, beaten

6 slices white toast, diced, or you
   can use croutons
1/2 lemon rind, grated

Boil beer, sugar, cinnamon, beaten egg yolks and lemon rind. Stir vigorously with wooden spoon while cooking. Boil 5 to 6 minutes, then simmer an additional 5 minutes. Dish over diced toast in bowls.

All I ask for is a chance to prove that money can't make me happy.
--Anonymous

Garlic Beer Soup

4 servings

Great if you have a stuffy nose!

1 (12 oz.) btl. beer (your choice) ☺
2 T. butter/olive oil
2 cans condensed beef broth
1 tsp. crushed red pepper; pizza pepper
1 tsp. black pepper
1 tsp. thyme
1 whole head garlic; cloves separated, peeled & chopped

Peel and chop the garlic. Heat the butter/oil over medium heat in a 2-quart pan. When butter foams, add the garlic and stir for only 1 or 2 minutes. Add the beef broth, beer and pepper and thyme. Raise heat, bring to a boil, reduce heat and simmer for a few minutes.

Dip fresh crusty bread in soup.

The problem with some people is that when they aren't drunk, they're sober.
--William Butler Yeats

Salads & Side Dishes

Seafood Salad

This is great for lunch or dinner when it is hot outside. Serve with cold beer or Long Island Iced Tea!

1 1/2 lb. crabmeat
1 1/2 lb. sm. shrimp, boiled in
  beer ☺ 3 to 5 minutes, peeled &
  veined
4 stalks celery, diced

1 jar black olives, chopped
1 jar pimentos, chopped
1 to 2 c. elbow or curly macaroni,
  cooked & drained

Mix all together with thousand island dressing.

Cranberry Salad

1 pkg. pineapple or orange Jello
1 (No. 2) can whole cranberries

1 tsp. grated orange rind
1 btl. ginger beer ☺

Combine Jello and cranberries in saucepan. Heat and stir until almost boiling and Jello is dissolved. Chill this mixture slightly. Carefully stir in ginger ale. When fizz stops, put entire mixture into a mold and chill until set.

Greeny Beany Potato Salad

If possible, use fresh ingredients, not canned!

1/2 c. Hellmann's mayonnaise
1/8 tsp. Tabasco sauce, to taste
1/2 tsp. salt
1 T. minced green onion
1 can green beans, drained, or
 fresh pre-cooked

1 can new potatoes, diced &
 drained, or cooked fresh & diced
2 T. beer ☺
Chopped celery, to taste

Mix all together and season to taste.

Pasta Salad

No beer in this one. (Drink a beer while preparing or a strong martini.) Great side dish for outdoor Bar-B-Q.

8 oz. spiral pasta or shell macaroni
Boiling water
6 oz. fresh mushrooms, sliced
1/4 c. rice vinegar
6 oz. sliced soft beer salami ☺
3 oz. sliced Genoa salami
3 oz. sliced hard salami or Italian
  salami
2 med. sweet bell peppers, diced

2 bunches green onions, sliced
  (about 2/3 c.)
6 oz. fresh spinach leaves, cleaned
  & stems removed
2 zucchini, about 4" long
1 c. crisp rice noodles or chow
  mein noodles
Oriental dressing

Cook pasta in boiling water until almost tender, about 10 minutes. Rinse and drain very well. Chill. Toss mushrooms with rice vinegar in large bowl or container. Cut the salami slice in quarters or bite-size pieces. Add salami, pasta, peppers and onions to the mushrooms. Do not mix. Remove stems from spinach, then wash. Roll single layer of leaves in paper towels to dry. Slice cucumbers. Mix together.

Beer and Spud Salad

3/4 c. mayonnaise
3/4 c. sour cream
1/3 c. beer ☺
6 to 8 c. cubed potatoes,
  pre-cooked

1 c. chopped onion
1 c. chopped celery
1/2 lb. bacon, cooked & crumbled
  (I use a whole pound of bacon!)

Blend mayonnaise, sour cream and beer. Toss with potatoes, onions, celery and bacon. Add salt and pepper to taste.

Serve cold or heated. Tastes great both ways!

Warning: The consumption of alcohol may make you think you can logically converse with other members of the opposite sex without spitting.
--Anonymous

Eggplant Pasta in Beer

A great one-dish meal. Can leave out ham for your vegetarian friends.

1/2 c. olive oil
1 med. eggplant, peeled & diced
Salt & pepper
6 oz. smoked ham, cubed
1 c. lager ☺
1 tsp. chopped fresh rosemary, or
   1/2 tsp. dried

1 c. fresh or frozen peas
1 lb. penne pasta, cooked
   according to the directions on the
   pkg.
Freshly-grated Parmesan cheese

In a large skillet, heat the olive oil over medium heat. Put in the eggplant and season with salt and pepper. Cook, stirring, for about 10 minutes, until it becomes soft. Stir in the ham and fry 2 minutes. Add the lager and rosemary and bring to a boil. Reduce the liquid by half. Put in the peas; reduce to a simmer, cover, and cook for 2 minutes. Stir the cooked pasta into the sauce and cook for 30 seconds to heat through. Transfer to a serving bowl, sprinkle with plenty of Parmesan cheese and serve.

An intelligent man is sometimes forced to be drunk to spend time with his fools.
--Ernest Hemingway

Hot German Potato Salad

6 to 8 servings

2 1/2 lb. red potatoes
1/2 c. finely-chopped mild red or
  yellow onions

1/4 c. finely-chopped parsley
2 T. chopped chives

BEER DRESSING:
6 T. olive oil
1/2 c. finely-chopped onions
3/4 c. lager beer ☺
3 T. malt or cider vinegar

1 T. Dijon mustard
1/2 tsp. sugar
Salt & pepper

  Cook the potatoes in boiling salted water until a knife point can be easily inserted, about 20 to 25 minutes. Remove and as soon as you can handle them, slice them, unpeeled, into 1/4-inch rounds. While the potatoes are still warm, gently mix them with the onions, parsley and beer dressing. Do not overmix or the potatoes may break into pieces. Taste for salt and pepper. Garnish with chopped chives. Serve warm. Also good at room temperature.

  Beer Dressing: Heat 2 tablespoons of the olive oil in a small frying pan over medium heat. Add the onions and cook just until soft, about 5 minutes. Add the lager, vinegar and sugar; boil for 5 minutes. Put into a food processor with the mustard. With the motor running, slowly pour in the remaining 4 tablespoons olive oil. Taste for salt and pepper.

Chicken Pasta Salad

4 servings

Great salad for lunch or lite dinner. There is no beer in this, so I guess you'll have to compensate by drinking a few. I am so very sorry!

3 c. dried pasta (bow-tie shapes or ziti)
4 T. med. hot mustard
2 T. brown sugar
3 T. extra-virgin olive oil
2 T. fresh lemon juice
1/4 tsp. salt

4 boneless, skinless chicken breast halves, cooked, cubed or sliced
3 celery stalks, sliced
2 c. seedless green grapes, halved
1/4 c. chopped walnuts
Salt & pepper, season to taste

Cook the pasta for approximately 15 to 25 minutes, or until pasta is (al dente) just tender. Drain well and set aside.

In a small bowl, mix the mustard, brown sugar, olive oil, lemon juice and salt. Set aside. In a separate large bowl, add the pasta and chicken. Coat with mustard dressing. Gently stir in the celery, grapes and walnuts.

We could certainly slow the aging process down
if it had to work its way through Congress.
--Will Rogers

Stuffed Fried Squash

8 to 10 servings

These are sooo------good!

**20 acorn squash or pumpkin
blossoms, stamen removed**

CHEESE FILLING:
4 oz. goat (Feta) cheese
4 oz. cream cheese
1/2 tsp. red pepper flakes
1/2 tsp. dried oregano

1/4 tsp. dried basil
1 clove garlic, minced
Salt & pepper, to taste

BEER BATTER:
1/8 c. cornstarch
1/2 c. flour
1/2 tsp. salt
1/2 tsp. black pepper
1/4 tsp. celery salt
1/4 tsp. baking soda
1/2 tsp. baking powder

1 egg, beaten
1/2 c. cold flat beer ☺
Vegetable oil, for frying
Salt & pepper, to taste
Grated Parmesan cheese & sliced
  olives, for garnish

Continued on following page.

Continued from preceding page.

Gently swish the squash blossoms in cold water to clean. Carefully twirl to remove most of the water, then drain thoroughly on paper towels. Set aside. Beat goat cheese, cream cheese, red pepper flakes, oregano, basil, garlic, salt and pepper until blended. Gently fill each blossom with about 2 teaspoons of the cheese filling. Refrigerate while making batter.

In a heavy skillet, heat 2 inches of oil to 375° over medium heat. While oil is heating, whisk together cornstarch, flour, salt, pepper, celery salt, baking soda, baking powder, egg and beer until combined.

Carefully dip a stuffed blossom into the batter, covering the entire flower and ease into the hot oil. Brown on one side, then turn to brown the other. Cook only a few at a time so they are not crowded. Remove with a slotted spoon and drain on paper towels. Repeat with remaining stuffed squash blossoms. Sprinkle stuffed squash blossoms with salt and pepper to taste and garnish with a sprinkling of grated Parmesan cheese and chopped chives.

Worrying is like a rocking chair; it gives you something to do,
but it doesn't get you anywhere.
--Anonymous

Southern Cooked Greens in Beer

1/2 lb. raw bacon, chopped	1 (12 oz.) btl. beer☺
3 c. julienne onions	1/4 c. rice wine vinegar
Salt	1 T. molasses
Freshly-ground black pepper	6 lb. greens, like mustard greens,
Pinch of cayenne pepper	collard greens, turnip greens,
3 T. minced shallots	kale & spinach, cleaned &
1 T. minced garlic	stemmed

In a large pot, cook the bacon until crispy, about 5 minutes. Add the onions and cook for about 6 to 7 minutes, or until the onions are wilted. Season the mixture with salt, pepper and pinch of cayenne pepper. Add the shallots and garlic; cook for 2 minutes. Stir in the beer, vinegar and molasses. Stir in the greens, a third at a time, pressing the greens down as they start to wilt. Cook the greens, uncovered, for about 1 hour and 15 minutes.

Only Irish coffee provides in a single glass all four essential food groups: alcohol, caffeine, sugar and fat.

--Alex Levine

Kickin' Beans

1 btl. dark beer ☺
Water, to cover beans (approx. 6 c.)
1 lb. dried pinto beans, cleaned &
  rinsed
1 sm. onion, chopped
6 slices bacon, cut into thirds

3 to 5 garlic cloves, minced
1 jalapeño chili, finely chopped
1 can minced chipotle chilies
Salt & pepper, to taste
Top with grated Cheddar cheese &
  chopped fresh cilantro

Put all ingredients in large pot. Simmer over low heat until beans are tender and liquid is reduced to cover beans by a little. Stir and add beer to pot as needed. Simmer for 2 or more hours. Salt and pepper to taste. Add cheese and cilantro.

Fried Asparagus

4 servings

This is a great side dish for beef, fish or chicken, or serve as an appetizer with hollandaise or your favorite sauce.

1/2 c. cornstarch	1/2 tsp. baking soda
3/4 c. flour	1 tsp. baking powder
1 tsp. salt	2 egg whites
1/4 tsp. black pepper	2/3 c. cold flat beer ☺
1/2 tsp. white pepper	3 lb. raw whole asparagus, cleaned
1/2 tsp. celery salt	& cut above white end

Mix all ingredients, except asparagus, in a bowl with a wire whisk until well blended. Dip asparagus stalks, one by one, in the batter and deep-fry them in at least 2 inches of peanut oil for 2 minutes, or until golden brown.

Be careful about reading health books. You may die of a misprint.
--Mark Twain

Carbo Beer Batter Baked Potatoes

Drink beer first so you won't think about the calories. Make batter first, an hour ahead of time.

4 baking potatoes, sm. to med.

1 c. corn flakes or similar cereal, crushed

BATTER:
1 1/2 c. flour
1 can beer (your choice) ☺

1 egg, separated
Salt & pepper, to taste

Beer Batter: Separate egg. Set aside egg white. Blend ingredients with mixer, using only the egg yolk. Let stand for 1 hour. Then beat egg white until stiff and fold into batter. Let stand for 1 hour before using.

Bake potatoes until nearly done (I do mine in the microwave). Dip in beer batter, roll in corn flake crumbs. Deep-fry until brown. Return to oven (325°) and bake until done.

Serve with your favorite condiments, you know, like lots of butter, sour cream, chives and grated cheese.

Maybe it's true that life begins at fifty ...but everything else starts to wear out, fall out or spread out.
--Anonymous

Warm Potato Salad

FOR THE POTATO SALAD:
2 to 3 lb. red potatoes
1/2 lb. bacon strips, cooked (not too crispy), drained & chopped
2 hard-boiled eggs, chopped
1 red onion, finely chopped
1 yellow onion, finely chopped
1/3 c. parsley, finely chopped
Chives (for garnish), chopped
Salt & pepper

FOR THE BEER DRESSING:
1 (12 oz.) btl. German lager ☺
Olive oil
4 T. cider vinegar
1 sm. yellow onion, finely chopped
1 clove garlic, finely chopped
1 T. Dijon mustard
1/2 tsp. sugar
Salt & pepper

Bring salted water to a boil. Add whole potatoes and cook for about 25 minutes, or until a knife can pierce the potatoes (do not overcook). Remove and let cool for a few minutes, then slice them into 1/4 round pieces. Gently mix in the onions, parsley, cooked bacon and eggs. Then mix in the beer dressing, taking care to not break the potatoes into small bits. Salt and pepper to taste, topping with chopped chives. Serve immediately; while still warm.

Beer Dressing: Heat some olive oil in a pan; medium heat. Cook the onion and garlic until soft. Add the beer, vinegar and sugar and boil for about 5 minutes.

Put the above and mustard into a food processor and process, while at the same time slowly blending in 5 tablespoons of olive oil (this will thicken the dressing). Salt and pepper to taste.

Red Cabbage

6 servings

Great with brats!

1 btl. lager ☺
1 head red cabbage, sliced into strips
1/3 c. apple cider vinegar
1 lg. onion, chopped

2 cloves garlic, minced
1 apple, cored & chopped
2 tsp. caraway seeds
Pepper, to taste
Olive oil

In pan with a lid, cook onions until clear and tender, about 5 minutes. Add apple and garlic and cook a little longer. Put in cabbage and add beer and apple cider vinegar. Stir in pepper. Add caraway seeds and cook for about an hour, covered.

First say to yourself what you would be; and then do what you have to do.
--Epictetus

Marinara Sauce with Beer

4 to 6 servings

1 c. pale ale ☺
2 lb. Roma tomatoes, quartered &
  simmered for 1 hour (reserve 1 c.
  of the water)
6 oz. tomato paste
1 clove garlic
1 tsp. fresh oregano

1 tsp. fresh basil
1 tsp. salt
1/2 tsp. fresh ground pepper
4 T. olive oil
1/2 c. diced yellow onion
Penne pasta

Heat olive oil in a 12-inch skillet over medium heat. Add onions and garlic and sauté for 2 minutes. Add tomatoes (with the 1 cup reserved water), tomato paste, ale, salt and pepper, basil and oregano. Reduce heat and simmer at least 30 minutes, stirring occasionally. Pour over cooked penne. Yum!

When I heated my home with oil, I used an average of 800 gallons a year. I have found that I can keep comfortably warm for an entire winter with slightly over half that quantity of beer.
                                        --Dave Berry

Sauerkraut Stuffing

12 cups

I've made this with chicken or turkey, and as a side dish for pork chops for something a little different.

1/2 to 3/4 lb. bacon, preferably thick cut, country-style, cut into 1/2" pieces (depends on how much bacon flavor you like)
2 c. chopped onion
2 c. chopped celery, including leaves
1 1/2 c. chopped carrots
1 T. chopped fresh thyme, or 1 tsp. dried
1 tsp. caraway seeds, lightly crushed

1 tsp. celery seeds
2 tsp. salt
2/3 c. beer ☺
2 c. chopped tart apples
8 to 10 c. stale or lightly-toasted 1/2" rye bread cubes
1 lb. fresh sauerkraut, rinsed & drained (usually sold in bags in deli section)
Freshly-ground black pepper, to taste

In a large skillet, fry the bacon over medium-high heat until crisp. Remove with a slotted spoon and set aside. Pour off all but 4 tablespoons of the bacon grease and set the pan over moderate heat. Add the onion, celery, carrots, thyme, caraway seeds, celery seeds and salt. Cook until the

Continued on following page.

Continued from preceding page.

vegetables begin to soften, about 10 minutes. Add the beer and bring to a boil, scraping the pan to loosen and dissolve the browned bits. Add the apples; cover and cook until the apples are tender. Remove from the heat and combine in a large bowl with the bread cubes and sauerkraut. (Make sure you rinse and drain sauerkraut.) Season with pepper; toss to combine.

Stuff the bird. Don't overstuff the bird. If baking some or all of the stuffing in a casserole, pour a cup or 2 of stock over the stuffing. Bake it covered until heated through, 45 minutes to 1 hour. For a crunchy top, uncover it for the last 15 minutes of baking.

Beer is proof that God loves us and wants us to be happy.
--Benjamin Franklin

Notes & Recipes

_____
_____
_____
_____
_____
_____
_____
_____
_____
_____
_____
_____
_____
_____
_____
_____
_____
_____
_____
_____
_____
_____

Marinades & Sauces

FAVORITE RECIPES
FROM MY COOKBOOK

Recipe Name	Page Number

Marinades & Sauces

Marinades

Beefy Steak Marinade

Enough for 2 steaks

1/2 c. beer ☺
1 T. lemon juice
1/4 tsp. dried thyme, basil,
  oregano, or your choice of herbs
1 to 2 tsp. Worcestershire sauce

1 tsp. soy sauce
1 tsp. honey or brown sugar
1 to 2 cloves garlic, to taste
Sprinkle some hot sauce, to taste

   Mix ingredients together and pour over steak. Cover both sides of steaks and refrigerate for an hour or more. Pour off marinade. Grill or cook in a pan.

I like beer. On occasion, I will even drink beer to celebrate a major event, such as the fall of communism or the fact that the refrigerator is still working.
                                                                --Dave Barry

Simple Steak Marinade

1 can beer ☺
1 stick butter
1 env. Lipton onion soup mix

1/4 tsp. garlic powder
2 T. steak sauce

Mix together. Pour over steaks. Grill. It's that simple. In other words, you can be stupid drunk and not screw this up. Just don't overcook the meat. Remember, the meat still cooks even after you take it off the grill.

Marinade for Pork Chops

This is going to clog your arteries, but tastes great.

2 to 4 pork chops
1 can or btl. beer ☺
1/4 to 1/2 tsp. cloves, crushed
3 to 4 slices cooked bacon

1 c. Tom Collins mix ☺
Liquid smoke, to taste
Caramel sauce
Butter, lots of it

Marinate pork chops in beer. Add crushed cloves and rest of ingredients. Brush with caramel sauce. Put a pat of butter or a stick on each chop. Grill chops, but don't overcook.

"Plumber-Butt" Marinade for Beef, Pork or Chicken

Even a simpleton can do this.

1 can beer, your choice ☺	1 doz. peppercorns
1/3 to 1/2 c. brown sugar	1 doz. cloves
1/3 c. soy sauce	1 tsp. ginger

Combine all ingredients. Pour over meat. Cover and refrigerate for several hours, or overnight, and go to local bar.

Beef Marinade

1 can or btl. beer ☺	1 T. sugar
1/2 c. salad oil or Italian dressing	1 tsp. salt
1 cloves garlic, smashed	3 to 4 whole cloves
2 to 3 T. lemon juice	

Combine beer with oil or salad dressing. Stir in a little at a time. Add the rest of the ingredients. Marinate beef. Pierce beef with fork and turn often. Put in refrigerate for at least an hour, or better, for several hours or overnight.

Chicky-Chick Marinade

Great for pork, too!

1 can or btl. beer ☺	4 to 6 scallions
1/3 c. orange or apricot marmalade	White & black pepper, to taste
1/3 c. teriyaki sauce	3 tsp. ginger powder
3 tsp. or more sugar, to taste	3 tsp. mustard powder
1/4 to 1/3 c. apple vinegar	Dash of hot sauce
4 to 6 cloves garlic	

Mix ingredients and pour over meat. Marinate several hours to overnight in refrigerator.

*A blond was fired from pharmacy job for failing to print labels...Helllloooo!!!
Bottles won't fit in typewriter!!!!!*

--Anonymous

Grass-Skirt Marinade

1 btl. Italian dressing (I use Zesty,
  but whatever is fine)
1 beer ☺
2 sm. or 1 lg. onion, chopped
3 to 4 T. chili powder
4 limes, juice only
2 to 3 T. fresh cilantro leaves,
  minced

2 to 3 T. lemon pepper seasoning
1 to 2 T. Worcestershire sauce
2 tsp. ground cumin
2 cloves garlic, smashed &
  chopped
1 to 2 tsp. cayenne pepper
1 to 2 bay leaves

Combine and pour over beef or chicken. If using both meats, put in separate containers to marinate. Serve with grilled onions, peppers and tortillas for fajitas.
    Yum!

Simple Chicken Marinade

1 can beer ☺
1/2 c. soy sauce
1 T. oil

2 cloves garlic, minced
2 T. onion, chopped
2 T. parsley, chopped

Marinate chicken pieces for several hours. Barbecue chicken pieces, brushing with sauce frequently.

71

Horseradish Beef Marinade

The horseradish makes this a great marinade.

1/2 c. olive oil
1 1/2 tsp. cayenne pepper
3 tsp. prepared horseradish
1/3 c. wine vinegar
2 tsp. spicy mustard
2 tsp. salt

2 cans lite beer ☺
2 tsp. chopped onion or onion
  powdered
1 clove garlic, or 2 tsp. garlic
  powder

Marinate for several hours, or overnight. Adjust seasonings to your own taste. Turn meat often for best results.

Golfers who try to make everything perfect before taking the shot rarely make a perfect shot.

--Anonymous

Sauces

Beef Slop

1 1/2 cups sauce

3 T. butter
1 lg. onion
1 c. chili sauce

1/2 c. beer ☺
1/2 c. sliced stuffed olives (opt.)

   Combine all ingredients in a saucepan and simmer for 10 to 15 minutes, or until flavors are blended.

God made man before woman so as to give him time
to think of an answer for her first question.
--Anonymous

A "Boat"-Load of Sauce

This recipe is great for a pig pickin' where you need a great deal of sauce for a large party, or if you want leftovers. Can put in bottles and give as gifts. Can freeze it as well! Adjust seasonings to taste.

1 lb. butter, melted

Add:
4 chopped onions

Cook until the onions are done.

Add the following ingredients:

2 gal. ketchup	**1/3 sm. btl. Worcestershire sauce,**
1 c. vinegar	**or more**
1 c. prepared mustard (can use hot	**1/2 sm. btl. lemon juice, or juice**
mustard for more kick)	**from 3 or more lemons**
1/3 sm. btl. hot sauce, to taste	**3 cans beer** ☺

Mix the following dry ingredients and add to the above:

2 (1 lb.) boxes dark brown sugar	**1 1/2 T. red pepper**
1/4 c. black pepper	**3 T. garlic powder**
1/4 c. salt	**3 T. celery seed**
2 T. chili powder	**3 T. sage**

Cook 45 minutes on medium heat. Stir often. Use a very heavy pan as this tends to burn.

In other words, if you don't like it and you have lots of leftovers, give it to your best friends!

Sa-weet Bar-B-Q Marinade and Sauce

If this isn't sweet enough for ya, add more honey or molasses and sugar!

1 c. barbecue sauce (your choice)
1 c. ketchup
2/3 c. beer (your choice) ☺
Honey or molasses
2 T. red wine vinegar
2 T. lemon juice

2 T. Dijon mustard
1 T. Worcestershire sauce
1 T. hot pepper sauce
1/2 tsp. pepper
2 to 3 cloves garlic, minced
2 onions, finely chopped

In a large bowl, combine all ingredients. Place food in marinade and refrigerate overnight, or let stand at room temperature for up to 2 hours. When ready to cook, remove food and place marinade in saucepan. Cook marinade on medium heat until thickened. Baste food with sauce while grilling.

A woman drove me to drink and I didn't even have the decency to thank her.
--W.C. Fields

"Sock-It-To-Ya" Barbecue Sauce

This one is a little spicy. Adjust seasonings to your taste. Can replace hot mustard for regular mustard.

1 (14 oz.) btl. ketchup
2/3 c. chili sauce
1/3 c. hot mustard
1 T. soy sauce
1/3 c. Worcestershire sauce
2 dashes Tabasco sauce

3/4 c. brown sugar
1/4 c. vinegar
1 T. lemon juice, fresh
1 tsp. pepper
1 T. vegetable oil
1/2 c. beer, or more ☺

In large saucepan, mix all ingredients together and cook on low for about 20 minutes.

This is great for rotisserie chickens or baby back ribs, etc. Just slop it on!

Golf is like marriage: If you take yourself too seriously it won't work, and both are expensive.

--Anonymous

"Road Kill" Bar-B-Q Sauce

5 quarts

Sorry about the name. This sauce will make shoe leather taste good. (Don't try it on shoe leather if you've had too much to drink. You'll be constipated for months.)

1 qt. tomato juice
1/2 c. Worcestershire sauce, or
  more, to taste
1 sm. jar mustard
1 (1 lb.) box brown sugar
1/2 c. pepper, or more, to taste
2 btl. catsup
2 btl. hickory barbecue sauce (any
  kind)

1 T. garlic salt
1/2 c. salt
1 (6 oz.) can tomato paste
1 pt. white vinegar
1 pt. salad oil
1 lg. onion, chopped
1 can beer ☺

Mix all ingredients in large saucepan; bring to a boil. Reduce heat; simmer for 1 hour.

WARNING: The consumption of alcohol may create the illusion that you are tougher, smarter, faster and better looking than most people.
--Anonymous

Strumin' and Drumin' Bar-B-Q Sauce

1 c. ketchup
2 cloves crushed garlic, or more
1 T. Italian spices, or a little
  oregano or basil
1 to 2 tsp. mustard
2 tsp. Worcestershire sauce

Dash of balsamic vinegar, or more,
  to taste
Several dashes of Tabasco sauce
Honey (to taste)
Ground black pepper
Splash of beer, or more ☺

Put everything in a jar and shake. Adjust seasonings to your taste.
Great on chicken and pork.

To some it's a six-pack, to me it's a Support Group.
--Anonymous

SSSSS-Spicy Citrus Barbie-Q Sauce

Lime juice and orange peel give this sauce a great citrus flavor.

1 (16 oz.) btl. any barbecue sauce
16 oz. beer (any kind) ☺
1 med. chopped onion
Dash of garlic juice
1 (2 oz.) ctn. lime juice (I use fresh
   lime in food & beer)

Dash of grated orange peel
Dash of pepper
A-1 sauce, to taste
Soy sauce, to taste
Heinz 57 sauce, to taste
Chili or red pepper, to taste

Combine all ingredients and simmer until all flavors blend together.

Chicken Lickin' Barbie-Q Sauce

3/4 c. oil
1/4 c. vinegar
2 eggs
1 tsp. onion powder
1 1/2 tsp. garlic powder
2 tsp. Worcestershire sauce

1/2 btl. Wish-Bone salad dressing
1 c. beer ☺
1 tsp. white pepper
1 1/2 tsp. poultry seasoning
1 tsp. salt
1 tsp. lemon juice

Mix all ingredients and marinate chicken for 3 to 4 hours, or overnight, if possible. Baste chicken often.

Ba, Ba, Baran... Beer Batter

Enough for 2 pounds of fish

This is a great batter for zucchini, squash, fresh asparagus and fish.

2 eggs, beaten	**3/4 tsp. salt**
2/3 c. beer ☺	**3 T. melted butter**
1 c. flour	**Fish or vegetables**

Beat egg yolks until smooth. Add beer, beat together. Gently stir in flour and salt until blended. Mix in butter and allow to stand at room temperature for 30 minutes. Beat egg whites until stiff; fold into flour mixture. Dip fish or vegetable pieces into mixture, drop into hot oil. Fry until lightly brown, drain on paper towel.

The secret of a good sermon is to have a good beginning and a good ending; and to have the two as close together as possible.
--George Burns

Seafood Marinade

Great with mild white fish.

1 btl. lager beer (your favorite) ☺	**1 to 2 tsp. Worcestershire sauce**
3/4 c. fresh lime juice	**1 tsp. soy sauce**
6 garlic cloves, minced	**1 T. hot sauce**
1 tsp. powdered chicken stock	**1 tsp. ground black pepper**

Add all ingredients and blend together. Let stand for an hour or two in refrigerator. Add fresh fish and marinate for 30 minutes or longer if possible.

You can use marinade during cooking.

I feel sorry for people who don't drink. When they wake up in the morning, that's as good as they're going to feel all day.
--Frank Sinatra

Notes & Recipes

Fish

FAVORITE RECIPES
FROM MY COOKBOOK

Recipe Name	Page Number

Fish

Coconut Beer Shrimp To Die For

1 lb. unpeeled med. fresh shrimp
3/4 c. pancake mix
3/4 c. beer ☺
1 T. coconut milk

1/4 c. all-purpose flour
1 c. coconut flakes
Light vegetable oil

Peel and devein shrimp; rinse well. Combine pancake mix, beer and coconut milk and mix well. Dredge shrimp in flour, shake off excess. Dip into batter, then dredge coated shrimp in coconut. Heat oil in saucepan (2-inch to 3-inch deep) to 350°. Fry 5 to 6 shrimp at a time approximately 35 to 45 seconds on each side and golden brown. Drain on paper towel and serve.

Don't worry about avoiding temptation as you grow older, it will avoid you.
--Winston Churchill

"Sand Trapped" Deep-Fried Shrimp

Make batter the day before when you are sober!

40 lg. shrimp	**6 T. melted butter**
3 c. cake flour	**2 1/4 c. flat beer ☺**
4 eggs, beaten	**Oil ,for deep-frying**
1 1/2 tsp. salt	

The day before: Measure out the beer and let it stand for an hour until it goes flat. Mix the flour, eggs, salt and butter together. Add the beer and mix again. Cover batter and refrigerate overnight.

The day of the meal: Shell and devein the shrimp. Rinse and pat dry with paper towels. Heat oil to 350°. Batter each shrimp and deep-fry a few at a time. Drain shrimp and place on baking sheet lined with paper towels in a very low oven (about 200°) while the rest of the shrimp is cooking.

The term "mulligan" is really a contraction of the phrase "maul it again."
--Anonymous

"Royal Flush" Hot Bar-B-Qued Shrimp

No lie, this is hot and spicy but works so well with plain rice and a salad. Can't handle heat, back off the peppers!

1 c. butter
1 onion, chopped
2 cloves garlic, minced
1 tsp. red pepper
1 tsp. black pepper
1/2 tsp. white pepper
1/2 tsp. crushed red pepper
1 tsp. ground cumin

1/2 tsp. thyme
1/2 tsp. rosemary leaves
1/4 tsp. oregano
1 T. Worcestershire sauce
1 lb. shrimp in shell
1/2 c. chicken broth
1/4 c. beer ☺

Melt 1/2 cup butter in large skillet. Add onion, garlic, peppers, cumin, thyme, rosemary, oregano and Worcestershire sauce. Cook 1 minute, stirring constantly. Add shrimp; cook 2 minutes, stirring. Add 1/2 cup butter and chicken broth. Cook 2 minutes, stirring constantly. Stir in beer and cook 1 minute.

Serve over rice or in bowls with sauce. French bread is good to dunk in sauce.

WARNING: The consumption of alcohol may lead you to think people are laughing WITH you.
--Anonymous

Fried Shrimp Marinade

1/3 c. Worcestershire sauce
1 c. lemon juice

1/2 tsp. salt
1/2 tsp. pepper

Place 20 to 36 medium or jumbo shrimp, peeled and deveined, in above marinade for 30 minutes. Dust lightly with plain flour. Then dip in beer batter and deep fry at 365° for about 5 to 7 minutes, or until golden brown.

BEER BATTER:
2 btl. beer ☺
2 c. flour

2 tsp. baking powder
12/ tsp. paprika

Shrimp 'N Beer Batter

1 c. sifted flour
1/2 tsp. sugar
1/2 tsp. salt
1 dash pepper
1 dash nutmeg

1 tsp. baking powder
1 beaten egg
1 c. beer ☺
2 lb. fresh shrimp
Cooking oil, for frying

Work the above ingredients, except for the shrimp, into a beer batter. Peel shell from shrimp, leaving the last section and tail intact. Cut almost through shrimp at the center back without cutting ends. Dry shrimp and dip into beer batter. Fry in deep, hot fat until golden brown; drain. Serve at once.

Beer Broiled Shrimp

3/4 c. beer ☺
3 T. oil
2 T. chopped parsley
4 tsp. Worcestershire sauce
1 clove minced garlic

1/2 tsp. salt
1/8 tsp. pepper
2 lb. lg. shrimp, shelled &
   deveined

Combine beer, oil, parsley, Worcestershire sauce, garlic, salt and pepper. Add shrimp and stir. Cover, let stand at room temperature for 1 hour. Drain, reserving marinade. Place shrimp on greased broiler rack and broil 4 to 5 inches from heat for 4 minutes. Turn and brush with marinade. Broil 2 to 4 minutes more, or until light pink.

Fried Fish in Beer Batter

This recipe uses cornmeal.

1 c. beer ☺
2 eggs
1/2 tsp. salt
1/4 c. cornmeal

1 tsp. paprika
1 tsp. baking powder
1 tsp. garlic powder
1 c. flour

In a bowl, combine all ingredients and mix well. Let mixture stand about a half hour before using. Dry fish well and dip in batter. Deep-fry for best results.

This batter can also be used for shrimp and scallops or any other seafood.

Light and Fluffy Beer Batter

Serves 6 to 8

1/2 c. cornstarch	1 c. beer ☺
1/2 c. flour	4 egg whites, stiffly beaten
1 tsp. salt	2 lb. fish fillets

   Combine cornstarch, flour and salt. Stir in beer and mix until smooth. Fold in beaten egg whites. Cut fish fillets into serving pieces and dip in batter. Fry in hot 375° oil until golden brown. Drain on paper toweling.

"Great Catch" Beer Batter Trout

   This recipe uses pancake flour.

Trout fillets	1 can beer ☺
Pancake flour	1 T. sugar
Salt	

   Open a can of beer in the morning so it is flat before evening use. Dry trout fillets on paper towels. Add enough pancake flour mix to 1 can beer to form a thin batter. (It will thicken on standing.) Add sugar and a dash of salt, and mix. Dip whole fillets or pieces in batter and fry very quickly in an inch of hot oil in a cast-iron skillet. Turn when brown, drain on paper towels and serve immediately.

Fish Beer Batter

This recipe uses Bisquick.

1 lb. fish fillets	**1 egg**
3 to 4 T. Bisquick baking mix	**1/2 c. beer** ☺
1/2 tsp. salt	**Soy sauce or vinegar**

Heat fat or oil (1-inch) to 350° in 2 1/2-inch deep, 12-inch skillet. Lightly coat fish with 3 to 4 tablespoons baking mix; set aside. Mix 1 cup baking mix, salt, egg and beer until smooth. Dip fish into batter letting excess batter drip into bowl. Fry fish about 2 minutes on each side, or until golden brown. Drain and serve hot with soy sauce or vinegar.

Work is the curse of the drinking classes.
--Oscar Wilde

"Bait and Tackle" Seafood Kabobs

8 servings

1/2 lb. butter
2/3 c. room-temp. beer, measured
  after foam subsides ☺
6 T. catsup
6 T. lemon juice
1/4 c. Worcestershire sauce
6 cloves garlic, crushed
1/4 tsp. salt

1/4 tsp. freshly-ground pepper
Sm. or lg. sea scallops (about
  1 1/4 lb.)
12 oz. swordfish or halibut steak
24 med. shrimp (about 1/2 lb.),
  peeled & deveined
1 lemon, thinly sliced

To make marinade, melt the butter over low heat in a medium saucepan. Stir in beer, catsup, lemon juice, Worcestershire sauce, salt, garlic, salt and pepper. Cool before using.

If the scallops are large, cut them in half. Cut the swordfish or halibut into 24 cubes, about 1/2-inch across. Place the seafood in a shallow glass dish, keeping each type separate. Pour the marinade over and toss the fish gently to thoroughly coat it. Marinate in the refrigerator 4 to 6 hours, turning occasionally. Thread the shrimp, scallops, swordfish or halibut, and lemon slices on 8 (15 to 18-inch) skewers, putting 3 pieces of each on a skewer. Broil or barbecue 4 to 5 minutes in a broiler or about 6 minutes on a barbecue. Turn the skewers, brush seafood with marinade, and broil 3 to 4 minutes or barbecue 6 minutes longer. Serve over rice or risotto.

Shrimp and Scallops with Pecan Rice

1/2 lb. unpeeled medium shrimp	1 T. cornstarch
1-10 1/2 oz. can beef broth	3/4 c. uncooked rice
1/3 c. beer ☺	1/4 c. chopped onion
1/2 lb. bay scallops	1/8 tsp. turmeric
1 clove garlic, minced	1 c. water
1/4 tsp. red pepper	1/4 c. coarsely-chopped pecans
2 T. butter	2 T. butter, melted

Peel and devein shrimp. Combine 1/2 cup broth and the beer in a shallow dish. Add fish. Cover and refrigerate 1 hour, stirring occasionally. Sauté pecans in 2 tablespoons melted butter until nuts brown. Remove with slotted spoon and set aside. Add rice, onion and turmeric to drippings and cook over medium heat, stirring constantly, for 1 minute. Add remaining broth and water. Bring to a boil. Cover, reduce heat and simmer 20 minutes, or until liquid is absorbed and rice is tender. Stir in pecans. Remove fish from marinade, reserving liquid. In skillet, add 2 tablespoons melted butter, fish, garlic and red pepper. Cook over medium heat for 2 to 3 minutes, or until fish is done, stirring frequently. Add cornstarch to reserved marinade, stirring well. Add to fish. Bring to boil and cook 1 minute, until slightly thickened. Stir constantly. Serve over the pecan rice.

"Champagnes of the north",
--Napoleon's army praising foamy wheat beers

"Lured" Grilled Tuna

1/2 c. fresh lime juice
1/2 c. beer ☺
4 tsp. cumin
1/2 tsp. salt
Fresh tuna fillets or steak for each
  person

Sliced avocado, salsa (opt.)
4 cloves garlic, minced
3 T. oil
4 tsp. Dijon mustard

Combine lime juice, beer, oil, cumin, mustard, salt and garlic in a large shallow dish. Marinate for 2 hours, turning occasionally. Cook on preheated grill, approximately 5 minutes each side.

Serve with salsa and a slice of avocado, if desired.

Sometimes when I reflect back on all the beer I drink, I feel ashamed. Then I look into the glass and think about the workers in the brewery and all of their hopes and dreams. If I didn't drink this beer, they might be out of work and their dreams would be shattered. Then I say to myself, "It is better that I drink this beer and let their dreams come true than be selfish and worry about my liver."

*   --Jack Handy*

Grilled Halibut or Fish Fillets

1/3 c. lime juice
3 cloves garlic, minced
1 T. polyunsaturated oil
1/3 c. beer ☺
1 T. parsley, chopped

1/2 tsp. cumin
2 tsp. Dijon mustard
Pepper, to taste
1 lb. halibut steaks or fillets

Place halibut in marinade dish and set aside. Combine remaining ingredients, pour over halibut. Cover and marinate in refrigerator for 1 hour, turning once. Drain halibut reserving marinade. Place on lightly-oiled grill, 4 to 5 inches from hot coals. Cook 4 to 5 minutes, baste with marinade and turn. Cook an additional 4 to 5 minutes, or until halibut flakes when tested with a fork.

Grilled Fish

Low-fat, healthy, and tastes great!

1 to 2 lb. fish fillets or steaks
1/3 c. lime juice
3 cloves garlic, chopped
1 T. oil

1/4 c. beer ☺
1 T. parsely, chopped
1 small jar hot salsa (or your taste)
Salt & pepper, to taste

To make marinade, combine lime juice, 3 cloves chopped garlic, oil, beer and parsley. Marinate fish 1 hour. Start grill. Grill fish 4 to 5 minutes per side, basting with marinade. Top with salsa and serve.

Baked Cod with Almonds

Can also use perch or orange roughy.

**Cod fillets (2 or more per person if
  small)
1/2 can beer** ☺

**1 stick butter
Lemon juice
Sliced almonds**

   Melt 1/4 stick of butter, add 1 ounce of beer and 1 ounce of lemon juice in a coffee cup for basting. Use the remaining butter to coat the entire inside of a glass baking pan. After coating the pan, pour in the remaining beer. Place individual fillets in pan. Place in oven at 325°. Once butter melts in pan, apply first basting coat of beer, juice and butter on top of the fillets. Bake for 5 more minutes and baste again. Add almond slices to the top of the fillets. Continue to bake until fish is flaky. Dab basting on fillets to keep them from drying out.

*You can't be a real country unless you have a beer and an airline.
It helps if you have some kind of a football team, or some nuclear weapons,
but at the very least you need a beer.*
                                          --Frank Zappa

Fried Scrod with Spicy Fruit Sauce

Scrod (1/2 lb. per 2 people)   Beer Batter (see recipe) ☺
Juice of 2 lemons   Parsley
Oil, for deep frying (vegetable)   Lemon wedges
1 c. flour   Spicy Fruit Sauce (see recipe)

Cut scrod into 2-inch pieces. Wash in cold water and sprinkle with lemon juice. Heat several cups of oil in a fryer or large saucepan until it reaches 375°. Dredge pieces of scrod in flour, then coat well with Beer Batter. Drop into boil, one by one. Do not crowd the fryer with too many at one time. Keep separated and cook until golden brown and crisp. Drain on paper towels. Garnish with parsley and lemon wedges. Serve with Fruit Sauce.

BEER BATTER:
1 (12 oz.) can light beer ☺   1 T. salt
1 c. flour   1 T. paprika

Mix flour, salt and paprika in a bowl. Slowly add beer while beating with a fork. Continue adding beer until batter is light and frothy. While using the batter, whisk from time to time to keep it mixed.

Continued on following page.

Continued from preceding page.

SPICY FRUIT SAUCE:
Makes 1 cup

3/4 c. orange marmalade
4 T. lemon juice
2 T. orange juice
2 tsp. horseradish

1/2 tsp. powdered ginger
1/2 tsp. salt
1/2 tsp. dry mustard (opt.)

Combine marmalade, lemon and orange juice in blender and purée until smooth. Pour into a bowl and add remaining ingredients. Mix well.

The Buffalo Theory of Beer Drinking and Brain Development
A herd of buffalo can only move as fast as the slowest buffalo, much like the brain can only operate as fast as the slowest brain cells. The slowest buffalo are the sick and weak so they die off first, making it possible for the herd to move at a faster pace. Like the buffalo, the weak, slow brain cells are the ones that are killed off by excessive beer drinking and socializing, making the brain operate faster.
The moral of the story: Drink more beer, it will make you smarter.

--Anonymous

Grilled Fiesta Fish Tuna with Salsa

4 servings

1 1/2 lb. tuna or firm-fleshed fish	1/4 c. beer ☺
1/3 c. lime juice	1/2 tsp. cumin
2 T. vegetable oil	Salt & pepper
3 cloves garlic	2 tsp. Dijon mustard
1 T. parsley	Salsa & avocado, to garnish

Combine all ingredients, except salsa and avocado. Pour over tuna. Cover and marinate in refrigerator. Drain tuna, reserving marinade. BBQ or boil 4 to 5 minutes, basting with marinade. Turn and cook another 4 to 5 minutes, until flaky. Serve with salsa and avocado.

SALSA:
Makes approximately 1 1/4 cups sauce

2 med. tomatoes, coarsely chopped	2 to 3 dashes liquid hot pepper
3 T. diced green chilies	sauce
1/4 c. chopped red onions	Salt

Combine all ingredients and blend well. Let stand at room temperature or in refrigerator for 15 to 20 minutes to blend flavors.

Fried Soft-Shell Crabs

3/4 c. unbleached white flour
2/3 tsp. salt
1 egg
2 tsp. fresh ginger, minced
3/4 c. beer (not lite beer) ☺

12 fresh med. soft-shell crabs
  (shelled & cleaned)
Corn, safflower or soy oil, for
  frying

In a small mixing bowl, combine first 4 ingredients and mix well. Add beer and mix well. Let batter stand at room temperature for a few hours.

Using a wok or heavy skillet at least 10 inches in diameter, add cooking oil. Heat oil to 375°. (turn heat to high--when a small piece of food dropped into oil sinks to bottom, sizzles, then rises to top--it is proper temperature). Turn heat to medium. Dip crabs in batter and fry 3 crabs at once, dropping them into oil, one at a time--careful of oil splattering. Fry only 1 minute. With tongs or slotted spoon, remove crabs and drain on paper towels.

When I read about the evils of drinking, I gave up reading.
--Henny Youngman

Poultry

FAVORITE RECIPES
FROM MY COOKBOOK

Recipe Name	Page Number

Poultry

"My Other Brother" Daryl's Chicken
(Easy Marinated Beer Chicken)

1 can or btl. beer ☺   **4 chicken breasts**

Place the chicken breasts in a plastic container. Pierce chicken with a fork and pour beer over the chicken. Put lid on container and put in refrigerator. Turn the chicken over after 30 minutes and throw on grill after marinating for 30 minutes to 1 hour. Do not <u>overcook</u>.

Life is too short to drink cheap beer.
--Anonymous

"Hammered" Fried Chicken

6 servings

This is great with potato salad or mashed potatoes and green beans. Yum!

1 3/4 c. sifted all-purpose flour	**1 (12 oz.) can beer** ☺
1 tsp. pepper	**Vegetable oil**
1 1/2 tsp. Season-All, Mrs. Dash or	**6 chicken breasts**
similar seasoning	

Combine sifted flour and pepper, Season-All (or similar seasoning) in medium bowl. Beat in beer with wire whisk or egg beater until smooth. Let stand 30 minutes. Pour vegetable oil in large skillet to equal 1-inch depth. Heat deep-fryer to 375° on thermometer, or until a cube of bread turns golden brown within 60 seconds.

Dip chicken pieces into beer batter one at a time. Let excess batter drain back into bowl. Fry chicken pieces, turning once, for 30 minutes, or until chicken tests done. Place chicken on paper towels to drain. Keep chicken warm in oven until all chicken is fried.

WARNING: The consumption of alcohol may cause you to tell the same boring story over and over again, until your friends want to smash your head in.
--Anonymous

"Cluckin Hooters"
(Chicken Breast Bake)

6 servings

3 whole chicken breasts, split	1/4 c. toasted slivered almonds,
4 to 5 T. all-purpose flour	divided
Salt & pepper, to taste	1/2 c. beer ☺
Salad oil	1 (3 oz.) can sliced mushrooms,
2 (10 3/4 oz.) cans cream of chicken	drained, or 1/3 c. cooked sliced
soup, undiluted	mushrooms
1 T. soy sauce	

Remove skin from the chicken; wash chicken and dry well with absorbent towels. Combine flour, salt and pepper. Dredge chicken in flour mixture and brown in heated oil. Place chicken in a shallow pan. Combine soup, soy sauce, 2 tablespoons almonds, beer and mushrooms; pour over chicken. Bake, uncovered, at 350° for 1 hour, basting occasionally. Sprinkle with remaining almonds.

WARNING: The consumption of alcohol may
leave you wondering where you left your clothes.
--Anonymous

Drunk Chicken

2 T. salad oil
1 (3 lb.) chicken, cut up
3 to 4 lg. tomatoes, cut up
1 (12 oz.) can beer ☺
1 tsp. oregano
1/2 tsp. pepper

3 garlic cloves, sliced
1 lg. onion, sliced
1 c. pimento-stuffed green olives
1 tsp. salt
1 bay leaf

In large skillet, heat oil over medium heat. Add chicken and garlic; cook until brown on all sides. Drain off fat. Add onion and continue cooking until translucent. Add remaining ingredients and bring to a boil. Cover; reduce heat and simmer 1 hour. Remove bay leaf. Serve over rice.

Time is never wasted when you're wasted all the time.
--Catherine Zandonella

Beer Batter Chicken

Flour and oil always make a mess, so if you cook, drink a lot for dinner and stagger over to the sofa or chair and pass out! Hopefully somebody else will clean up the mess!

2/3 c. all-purpose flour	1 egg
1 tsp. salt	Salad oil
1/2 tsp. double-acting baking powder	1 (3 lb.) broiler-fryer chicken, cut up
1/3 c. beer ☺	

In a bowl with a fork, mix first 3 ingredients. In another bowl, beat together beer, egg and 2 teaspoons salad oil; stir liquid into flour mixture. Coat half of chicken pieces with batter.

In a 12-inch skillet over medium heat, heat 1/2 inch salad oil to 370°. Fry chicken pieces until browned and tender, about 20 minutes, turning once. Drain on paper towels.

Golf! You hit down to make the ball go up. You swing left and the ball goes right. The lowest score wins. And on top of that, the winner buys the drinks.
--Anonymous

Barbeque Turkey Drumsticks

1 (2 1/2 lb.) pkg. frozen turkey
  drumsticks, defrosted
1 c. barbeque sauce
1/2 c. beer ☺

1/4 tsp. salt
1/8 tsp. pepper
Spiced peaches (can use canned
  peaches, smashed)

Arrange turkey in baking dish. Mix barbeque sauce, spiced peaches, beer, salt and pepper. Pour over drumsticks. Cover tightly and microwave on HIGH 10 minutes. Turn drumsticks over. Cover tightly and microwave on MEDIUM for 25 minutes. Turn drumsticks again and cover. Microwave until meat feels very soft when pressed, 25 to 40 minutes.

A blond baked a turkey for 4 1/2 days...instructions said
1 hour per pound and I weigh 108!
--Anonymous

"Prize Fightin" Beer Batter Chicken with Onions

6 servings

4 lb. chicken parts

1 lg. Bermuda onion (1 lb.)

BEER BATTER:
2 c. buttermilk baking mix
1 tsp. onion powder
1 tsp. garlic powder

1 lg. egg, room temp., separated
1 (12 oz.) can beer ☺

Sprinkle chicken with 1 tablespoon salt and 1 1/2 teaspoons pepper; set aside. Peel onion, cut crosswise into 1/4-inch slices. Separate into rings; set aside.

Beer Batter: In large bowl, mix baking mix with onion and garlic powders. Stir in egg yolk and beer until blended. In small bowl, use electric mixer at high speed, beat egg white until stiff; with rubber spatula, fold into batter.

In 5-quart Dutch oven, heat 2 inches salad oil over medium-high heat until 375° on deep-fat thermometer. Preheat oven to 350°.

Dip several chicken pieces into batter; shake off excess. Fry 10 minutes, turning once, until chicken is deep golden brown. Remove chicken to wire rack set on large baking sheet. Keep warm in oven while coating and frying remaining chicken.

Place onion rings in remaining batter; toss well to coat. With long fork, lift out a few onion rings. Drain off excess batter. Fry 6 minutes, turning once, until deep golden brown. With slotted spoon, remove onion rings to paper towel-lined wire rack set over large baking sheet; keep warm in oven while frying remaining onion rings. Serve chicken and onion rings.

Goose Your Chicken

Since this recipe has been out awhile and has had several revisions, there is a special pan just for this chicken recipe available at many cooking stores including Williams and Sonoma. However, you don't need a special pan.

Favorite rub, homemade or store-
bought works
1 whole chicken

1 can beer, regular or tall-size is
easier ☺
Olive oil
Salt & pepper

Pour out or drink some of the beer (about 1/4 of it). Clean chicken and wash thoroughly. Pour olive oil over chicken, rubbing all areas. Smear rub on chicken and put some in beer. The beer is going to foam. This is normal. Goose the chicken with the beer can. Put in a pan with some water/beer in pan or some people, put the chicken directly on the grill. I like to use an old pan. Move the legs until it stands on its own. Cook the chicken with lid down on grill until done. The skin will be clear or use a thermometer to make sure it is done.

RUB MIX:
Garlic, mashed
Fresh basil
A little cayenne pepper

A little brown sugar (opt.)
Salt & pepper, to taste

Can also use store-bought. Usually sold in seasonings area.

"Birdied" Chicken Pot Pie

6 servings

SHELL:
2 c. finely-crushed Club or Town House crackers

4 T. melted butter

In a 4x9-inch pan, pour the melted butter into the casserole dish, sprinkle the cracker crumbs over the butter and mix well to saturate the crackers. Press down cracker mix to cover the bottom evenly. Place, covered, into refrigerator while preparing the chicken.

FILLING:
1 (2 lb.) chicken, sliced 1" cubed
1 bag frozen mixed vegetables
2 T. olive oil
1 btl. beer ☺
1 tsp. poultry seasoning
1 1/2 tsp. garlic powder

1 tsp. basil
1 tsp. Lipton onion soup mix
1 can condensed cream of potato soup
2/3 c. milk
1 tsp. salt (opt.)

Add the olive oil to a frying pan with the poultry seasoning, garlic powder, basil and onion soup mix, and stir until well saturated with oil. Add chicken and brown lightly. Add the beer, cream of potato soup and milk when chicken looks golden brown. Add the frozen vegetables and turn down the heat to reduce the liquids for approximately 20 minutes. Remove from heat when liquids appear thickened. Allow to cool to warm to the touch.

Continued on following page.

Continued from preceding page.

CRUST:

2 c. flour

3/4 c. Crisco

1 tsp. salt

1/4 c. boiling water

1 tsp. parsley flakes

Add dry ingredients to hot water and milk. Cut Crisco into flour and milk mixture with knife or fork. Form into ball (minimize touching with hands). Divide ball in half. Roll out dough between sheets of waxed paper or plastic wrap to 1/8-inch thin.

Remove the casserole dish from the refrigerator and add the chicken filling. Peel the plastic wrap off of one side of the crust, fold dough over the dish and remove the other sheet of plastic wrap. Pinch sides of dough into the inside edge of the dish with fingers. Use a knife to poke several vent holes in crust. Bake at 425° for 20 to 25 minutes, until crust is golden brown over a cookie sheet.

Golf is the only sport where the most feared opponent is you.
--Anonymous

"No. 2 Handicap" Chicken 'n' Rice

4 to 6 servings

This is a Spanish dish. Very good!

3 lg. cloves garlic, crushed
1 tsp. salt
1 chicken, cut into 8 serving pieces
 (or I use pick of the chick)
2 T. oil
1 med. red onion, chopped
1 med. green bell pepper, seeded
 & chopped
2 bay leaves
1 tsp. ground cumin
1 T. sweet paprika
1 tsp. oregano

Juice of 1 lime
1/2 tsp. white pepper (or more, to
 taste)
1 c. tomato sauce
1 c. beer ☺
2 c. rice
2 c. chicken stock
1 c. cooked green peas
2 red bell peppers, roasted & cut
 into strips
1/3 c. pitted, coarsely-chopped
 green olives

To make marinade, mash the garlic and salt to a paste. Stir in lime juice. Rub chicken pieces with this mixture, marinating for at least 2 hours.

Heat 1 tablespoon oil in a large skillet with a lid and sauté chicken pieces, skin-side first, until golden brown, about 6 minutes on each side, and transfer to a plate. Sauté the onion until clear, about 3 minutes, adding oil, if needed. Add green pepper and seasoning, and sauté for 2 minutes. Stir in tomato sauce and beer. Add the chicken pieces and simmer over medium heat for 5 minutes. Stir in the rice and half of the stock. Bring to a boil over medium heat. Reduce to a simmer, covered, and cook until rice is tender, about 25 minutes, adding more liquid as required. Carefully mix in green peas, adjust seasoning and arrange on a large platter. Garnish with roasted red peppers and green olives.

You Callin' Me Chicken?

(Slow-Cooked Chicken)

1/2 btl. beer ☺
1 red pepper, diced
1 green pepper, diced
1 lg. can tomatoes
Chicken breasts, skinned

1 sm. can green or black olives, diced (save juice & add to mixture)
1 med. to lg. onion, diced
1 clove garlic, mashed
1 sm. to med. can mushrooms (save juice & add to mixture)

Put chicken in crock-pot. Add all ingredients. Put on low and cook all day, or medium for 3 to 4 hours, until done.

How does a man keep his attractive, blonde wife at home?
He puts in a circle driveway!

Chicken Baked Chicken

3 lb. fryer parts, cut up (breasts
  should be halved)
2 pkg. Good Seasons Italian salad
  dressing mix (dry)
3 T. flour
2 tsp. salt
1/4 c. lemon juice or white vinegar

2 T. melted butter
Oil, for deep frying
1 c. milk or beer ☺
1 1/2 to 2 c. pancake mix
1 tsp. paprika
1/2 tsp. powdered sugar
1/4 tsp. pepper

Make a paste of dry dressing, flour, salt, lemon juice and butter. Coat chicken with paste. Cover and marinate at least 2 hours. One hour before serving, heat enough oil in a 9-inch heavy pan to a 3-inch depth to 425°.

Mix pancake mix with paprika, sage and pepper. Dip chicken pieces in milk, then pancake mix. Let each piece dry for 4 to 5 minutes. Fry in hot oil without turning, for 5 to 6 minutes. Remove carefully and place on shallow baking pan. Dot not let pieces touch. Bake at 350° for 25 to 30 minutes.

*WARNING: The consumption of alcohol may cause you
to tell your friends over and over again that you love them.*
—Anonymous

"High Fly" Chicken Chili

2 lb. boneless chicken breasts, cubed
3 (15 oz.) cans kidney beans, drained
3 T. green chilies, chopped (opt.)
1 env. onion soup mix

1 (8 oz.) can tomato sauce
1 c. beer ☺
1 1/2 T. chili powder
2 pkg. cornbread mix
1 c. Cheddar cheese, shredded

Combine chicken, beans and chilies. Stir in onion soup mix, blended with tomato sauce, beer and chili powder. Bake, covered, 1 1/2 hours at 350° (or until chicken is tender). Prepare cornbread. Stir in cheese, spoon onto chili. Continue baking 25 minutes, until cornbread is golden. Serve <u>hot</u>.

For juicier chili, don't drain the beans. Also, you may use boneless chuck steak instead of chicken.

Billy Bob's Bar-B-Q Chicken

2 T. spicy mustard
2 T. apple vinegar
1 btl. Zesty Italian salad dressing
1/2 c. green onions, sliced
6 chicken breasts

1/8 tsp. garlic powder
1/4 tsp. lemon pepper
2 T. brown sugar
1/2 can warm beer ☺

Skin and pierce chicken breasts. Combine above ingredients and marinate chicken in refrigerator for 8 hours. Grill at 300° for 1 1/2 hours, turning frequently and basting with marinade.

Beef, Veal,
Lamb & Game

FAVORITE RECIPES
FROM MY COOKBOOK

Recipe Name	Page Number

Beef, Veal, Lamb & Game

Beef

"Blitzed" Marinated Steak

1 cold beer (your choice) ☺   **1/2 to 1 btl. Italian dressing (I use zesty, but any will do)**

Steaks: Depending on how large or how many steaks you have, adjust amount of beer and dressing to cover. Put steaks in a plastic container with a lid. Pierce the steaks with a knife and add beer, dressing and pepper if you like (no salt). Put in refrigerator for 15 to 20 minutes while getting coals ready. Flip steaks in marinade. Put back in refrigerator for another 15 to 20 minutes. Cook steaks on grill.
Da-lish!

You're not drunk if you can lie on the floor without holding on.
--Dean Martin

Coffee Encrusted Steaks

4 servings

12 oz. dark beer ☺
1/4 c. Worcestershire sauce
1 T. Tabasco sauce
4 boneless strip streaks (1 1/2 to
  2 lb. total), trimmed of fat
3 T. fine-ground espresso or dark
  roast coffee

1 T. pure chili powder
1 tsp. ground cumin
1 tsp. sugar
1/2 tsp. cayenne, or more, to taste
1 tsp. salt
1/2 tsp. fresh-ground black pepper

The night before, mix beer, Worcestershire sauce and Tabasco sauce in large freezer-weight zip-seal plastic bag. Put steaks in bag, seal and refrigerate overnight.

The next day, mix remaining ingredients in small bowl. Remove steaks from marinade and discard marinade. Pat steaks dry with paper towels, then scatter spice mix over steaks, patting it in with your fingers.

Preheat gas or charcoal grill to high and let rack get good and hot. Brush and oil rack, then grill steaks until darkly crusted and done the way you like, about 3 minutes per side for medium rare (about 145° on an instant-read thermometer) or 4 to 5 minutes per side for medium (about 160° on an instant-read thermometer). Let meat rest off heat 5 minutes to redistribute juices.

"Touch Down" Steak

6 to 8 servings

3 lb. sirloin steak
12 oz. beer ☺
1/2 c. chili sauce
1/4 c. salad oil
2 T. soy sauce
1 T. prepared mustard

1 med. onion, chopped
2 cloves garlic
1 1/2 tsp. salt
1/2 tsp. pepper
1/2 tsp. Tabasco sauce

Combine all ingredients, except steak. Simmer for a few minutes. Brush both sides of steak with sauce; grill steak 4 inches from medium-hot coals. Turn. Baste with extra sauce and broil other side.

Marinated Steak

4 to 6 servings

1 can beer ☺
1/2 c. chili sauce
1/4 c. salad oil
2 T. soy sauce
1 T. Dijon mustard

Tabasco sauce, to taste
1 T. liquid smoke, to taste
1 med. onion, coarsely chopped
Garlic, salt & pepper
3 lb. sirloin steak

Mix ingredients and simmer 30 minutes. Marinate steak overnight. Grill steak 15 minutes on each side while basting it with sauce. Serve steak with remaining sauce (cut sirloin in long diagonal slices).

Bag It Bar-B-Qued Steak

4 servings

1 1/2 lb. beef sirloin steak, about
  3/4" thick
1 (7 oz.) can beer ☺
1 med. onion, finely chopped

1/2 c. soy sauce
1/4 tsp. black pepper
1/4 c. shredded Cheddar cheese

    Place steak in plastic bag. Combine beer, onion, soy sauce and pepper; pour over steak. Press air out of bag; tie top securely. Refrigerate 8 hours, or overnight, turning over occasionally. Remove steak from marinade and place on grill 4 to 5 inches from hot coals. Cook 7 to 10 minutes on each side, or to desired degree of doneness; sprinkle cheese evenly over top side of steak during last few seconds of cooking time.
    To serve, cut across grain into thin slices.

WARNING: The consumption of alcohol may cause you to thay shings like thish.
--Anonymous

Beef Tenderloin and Mushroom Gravy

6 to 8 servings

4 to 5 lb. beef tenderloin, deveined   **Italian salad dressing**

GRAVY:
1 box mushrooms, sliced   **Worcestershire sauce**
Butter   **1 jar brown gravy (can use store-**
Flour   **bought or make your own)**
1/2 can beer ☺

Brush beef tenderloin with Italian salad dressing. Bake at 450° for 45 minutes.

Meanwhile, sauté mushrooms in a little butter. Sprinkle a little bit of flour on top and blend. Add beer and a little Worcestershire sauce. Blend. Add jar of brown gravy.

Heat and serve with tenderloin.

Barbecue Brisket

3 to 4 lb. beef brisket   **3/4 c. beer** ☺
1 pkg. Adolph's meat marinade   **3/4 c. ketchup**

Pour marinade over brisket. Prick with fork; after 15 minutes, turn over, prick and leave in marinade another 15 minutes. Drain, place in roaster and cover with beer and ketchup. Cover pan and place in oven at 300° for 3 to 4 hours. Cool, slice and reheat.

"How About That" Beef, Beer, Wine and Sherry

10 to 12 servings

Make ahead.

5 lb. sirloin tip roast	**1/2 tsp. salt**
1 (12 oz.) can beer ☺	**1/2 tsp. pepper**
4 T. flour	**1/2 tsp. onion salt**

WINE MARINADE:

1/2 c. salad oil	**1/2 tsp. salt**
1/4 c. red wine vinegar	**1/4 tsp. onion salt**
1/2 c. tomato purée	**1/4 tsp. garlic salt**
1/2 c. sherry ☺	**Pinch of pepper**
1/4 c. Burgundy ☺	

Place roast in large plastic bag and add beer. Close tightly and refrigerate for at least 12 hours. When ready to prepare, preheat oven to 325°. Remove roast from plastic bag, reserving beer marinade.

Rub roast with flour, salt, pepper and onion salt. Place in large roasting pan and add beer marinade to pan. Bake about 1 1/2 hours, or until meat thermometer reads 140°. Baste often with pan drippings.

Combine ingredients for wine marinade. Mix well and set aside. Slice the cooled roast very thin. Place in large casserole and pour wine marinade over meat. Cover and refrigerate about 12 hours. When ready to serve, if desired, serve warm with marinade heated and poured over meat.

"7th Inning Stretch" Slow-Cooked Pot Roast with Dried Fruit

6 servings

2 onions, sliced
3 to 4 lb. boneless pork roast
1 (11 oz.) pkg. mixed dried fruit
3/4 c. beer ☺
1 c. water
1 clove garlic, minced

1/4 c. brown sugar, tightly packed
1 bay leaf
1/4 tsp. cinnamon
2 1/2 tsp. salt
1/4 tsp. pepper
Spiced apple rings

Place sliced onions on bottom of slow-cooker. Place roast on top of onions (cut to fit pan). Cover with dried fruit. Mix remaining ingredients, except apple rings, and pour over roast. Cover and cook on low setting 6 to 8 hours. Top with spiced apple rings and serve.

Great with mashed potatoes and green beans.

Golf is harder than baseball. In golf, you have to play your foul balls.
--Anonymous

Braised London Broil

6 servings

Awesome flavor for inexpensive meal.

2 1/2 to 3 lb. London broil, cut at least 1" thick
1/2 tsp. kosher salt
1 tsp. freshly-ground black pepper, or more
3 to 4 T. cornstarch
1/4 tsp. dried thyme
1/4 strip uncooked bacon, cut into 6 (1/4") pieces

1 lg. clove garlic, peeled & cut lengthwise into 6 slivers
1 lg. onion, sliced 1/4" thick
1 bay leaf
1 c. stout or dark ale ☺
1 1/2 T. honey
2 T. red wine vinegar
1 T. Worcestershire sauce

Preheat oven to 275°. Trim London broil of any fat. Sprinkle meat on both sides with half the salt and pepper. Dredge the meat in the cornstarch, and pat the cornstarch into the beef. Sprinkle thyme over bacon and press firmly into the bacon pieces. With a sharp knife, cut 6 gashes, evenly spaced, across the meat. Push 1 piece of bacon and 1 sliver garlic into each gash in the meat. Place London broil in a lightly-oiled heavy pot or ovenproof casserole. Arrange onion slices on top of meat.

Combine bay leaf, stout beer, honey, red wine vinegar, and Worcestershire sauce, stirring to combine. Pour mixture over the top of the

Continued on following page.

Continued from preceding page.

onions. Sprinkle with remaining salt and pepper. Place a layer of heavy-duty foil over the top of the pot, and cover tightly with a lid. Bake 3 hours without peeking. Do not remove lid! When done, remove from oven and let rest at least 15 minutes. Carve into slices cut against the grain and place on serving platter. Cover with half of the pan juices.

Can thicken rest of pan juices to make gravy. Serve with mashed potatoes, wide noodles, or rice and a vegetable.

Easy Beef 'n Beer

4 to 6 servings

Need a Brown and Serve cooking bag.

Chuck roast	**4 med. onions, cut up**
Garlic salt	**1 (12 oz.) can beer** ☺
Cooking bag	**1 (10 1/2 oz.) can beef bouillon**

Salt roast with garlic salt and place in cooking bag. Add onions around roast and pour in beer and bouillon. Close bag and piece top. Cook at 350° for 1 1/2 to 2 hours, depending on size of roast.

Beef 'n Brewsky

10 to 12 servings

Make ahead. Need a cooking bag.

1 (5 lb.) sirloin roast	**1/2 tsp. onion salt**
1 (12 oz.) can beer ☺	**1/8 tsp. pepper**
1/4 c. flour	**1/4 c. salad oil**
1/4 tsp. salt	**1 Brown & Serve bag**

Put roast in Brown and Serve bag. Add beer. Place in refrigerator overnight, or for 12 hours. Next day, preheat oven to 325°. Remove roast from bag and reserve beer. Combine flour, salt, garlic, onion salt and pepper. Rub over meat. Insert meat thermometer and place roast on rack in roasting pan. Roast, uncovered, 1 hour and 50 minutes, basting roast every 15 to 20 minutes with salad oil and 1/2 cup reserved beer. When finished cooking, let roast cool completely.

MARINADE:

1/2 c. salad oil	**1/2 tsp. salt**
1/4 c. red wine vinegar	**1/4 tsp. onion salt**
1/2 c. tomato purée	**1/4 tsp. garlic salt**
1/2 c. Burgundy wine ☺	**1/8 tsp. pepper**
1/2 c. dry sherry ☺	**1/2 c. marinara sauce**

Combine marinade ingredients. Slice roast very thin and place in marinade. Refrigerate overnight.

Serve as sandwiches or warm with marinade heated and poured over meat.

German Pot Roast

1/2 lb. bacon
5 lb. chuck roast
1/4 c. vegetable oil
1 1/2 c. chopped onion
1 1/2 c. chopped carrot
2 stalks celery, chopped
5 cloves garlic, chopped
1 qt. water
2 btl. stout beer☺
2 btl. high-quality lager beer☺
1/8 c. beef bouillon granules

1/2 c. Dijon mustard
3/4 c. molasses
6 sprigs fresh sage
6 sprigs fresh thyme
6 sprigs fresh parsley
1 to 2 lb. turnips, cut & diced
1 to 2 lb. carrots, cut & diced
1 to 2 lb. rutabagas, cut & diced
2 lb. potatoes, peeled, cut & diced
Fresh rosemary, thyme & sage
   sprigs, for garnish

Cook bacon over medium heat in large ovenproof pot until fat has rendered, 3 to 5 minutes. Remove bacon, chop and set aside. In a separate pan, brown roast on all sides in the vegetable oil.

To the rendered bacon fat in the pan, add onion, carrot, celery and garlic. Cook until wilted and lightly browned. To the cooked vegetables, add water, beers, bouillon, mustard, molasses, sage, thyme and parsley. Bring to a boil and place meat in pot with vegetables. Cut a piece of parchment paper to fit over the pot and place it on top of mixture. Cover pan tightly with foil. Roast in oven at 375° for 1 1/2 to 2 hours. Allow to cool, then skim fat. Remove roast and set aside. Simmer vegetables in cooking liquid until crisp tender.

Garnish and serve with horseradish sauce.

This is great with fresh rolls or bread and apple butter.

Beef, Brew and Cabbage

The beer makes a rich broth without tasting like beer.

3 to 5 lb. fresh beef brisket
2 (12 oz.) btl. lager beer ☺
2 c. water (or enough to cover)
2 bay leaves
12 black peppercorns
1/2 c. chopped parsley
2 tsp. salt
2 T. olive oil
3 cloves garlic, peeled & sliced

2 c. chopped & rinsed leeks (white parts only)
2 med. yellow onions, peeled & sliced
3/4 lb. lg. carrots, cut into lg. pieces
3/4 lb. sm. red potatoes
1 lb. turnips, peeled & quartered
2 lg. green cabbages, quartered
Salt & freshly-ground black pepper, to taste

In a large pot with lid, on the burner, add the beef, beer, water, bay leaves, peppercorns, parsley and salt.

Heat a frying pan and add the olive oil. Sauté the garlic, leeks and yellow onion for a few minutes and add to the pot. Cover the pot and simmer gently 3 1/2 hours, or until the meat is very tender. (This will normally take about 1 hour per pound of brisket.) In the last 25 minutes of cooking, add the carrots and red potatoes. In the last 15 minutes of cooking, add the turnips, cabbage, salt and pepper.

If the vegetables are not done, cook them longer, but do not overcook.

Italian Stallion Beef

Make ahead. Great recipe for a picnic or when you are expecting guests and want to have food in refrigerator. Yummy.

4 to 5 lb. beef roast	**2 (10 1/4 oz.) cans onion soup**
Oregano	**1 btl. beer (not lite)** ☺
Pepper	**2 (2 oz.) shots of bourbon** ☺

Rub roast with oregano and pepper (no salt). Use enough to cover it all over. Place in open pan, uncovered, and bake at 500° for 1 hour. Take out and cool overnight in a refrigerator. Slice beef thinly and place a layer of beef in the bottom of a deep, covered pan. Add on top 1 can onion soup, 1/2 bottle beer and one shot of bourbon. Repeat another layer until roast is gone. Cover and bake at 300° for 4 hours.
Serve on rye or wheat buns.

Give me golf clubs, fresh air, and a beautiful partner,
and you can keep my golf clubs and the fresh air.
--Jack Benny

"Punt It" Pot Roast

6 to 8 servings

4 to 5 lb. beef chuck roast, boneless	2 T. flour
1 T. salad oil	1 (12 oz.) can beer ☺
4 med. onions, sliced	1 T. brown sugar
2 T. butter	1 T. vinegar
1 1/2 tsp. salt	2 T. parsley
	1 lg. clove garlic, minced

Using a heavy large pot with lid, brown meat in oil on both sides. In a separate pan, sauté onions in butter until pale golden color. Sprinkle with flour and cook for 2 minutes. Pour in beer and bring to a boil, stirring all the time. Then pour over the meat. Add brown sugar, vinegar, garlic and salt. Cover and simmer 2 to 2 1/2 hours, or until meat is tender. Lift meat onto a hot platter, sprinkle with parsley and keep warm. Cook down pan juices with the onions until slightly thickened. Add slices of roast and serve.

If your best shots are the practice swing and the "gimme putt",
you might wish to reconsider this game.
--Anonymous

Two-Fisted Stroganoff
Steak Sandwiches

6 servings

It's gonna to take 2 hands to eat this. Yum!

2/3 c. beer ☺	**1 T. butter**
1/3 c. oil	**1/2 tsp. paprika**
1 tsp. salt	**4 c. sliced onions**
1/4 tsp. garlic powder	**12 slices toasted French bread**
1/4 tsp. pepper	**1 c. sour cream, warmed**
2 lb. flank steak (1" thick)	**1/2 tsp. horseradish**

Combine beer, oil, salt, garlic powder and pepper in shallow dish. Place flank steak in marinade and cover. Marinate overnight in refrigerator. Drain and grill approximately 5 minutes on each side for medium rare.

Melt butter in frying pan. Add paprika and dash of salt. Add onions and cook until tender but not brown. Thinly slice meat on diagonal across grain. For each serving, arrange meat slices over 2 slices French bread. Top with onions. Combine sour cream and horseradish. Spoon atop each sandwich. Sprinkle with paprika.

Golf is the most fun you can have without taking your clothes off.
--Chi Chi Rodriguez

Napoleon-Style Ribs
(Short and Mighty)

3 or 4 lb. meaty beef short ribs
1 1/2 c. favorite dark beer ☺
3 T. brown sugar
3 T. vinegar
3/4 c. chili sauce

1 tsp. dry mustard
1/2 tsp. chili powder
1/2 tsp. paprika
2 med. onions, sliced

Preheat oven to 300°. Brown ribs in hot oil in heavy skillet. Do not allow ribs to touch; brown on all sides. Transfer ribs to heavy large pot with lid; add onions. De-glaze skillet with 1/2 cup beer. Add to pot. Combine all other ingredients and pour over ribs and onions. Cover tightly and bake for 2 1/2 to 3 hours. Add more beer only if necessary to moisten sauce. Sauce can be thickened with cornstarch, if desired.

Serve with noodles or boiled potatoes.

WARNING: The consumption of alcohol is a major factor in dancing on top of a table.
--Anonymous

1st and Goal Short Ribs with a Kick

8 servings

8 lb. beef short ribs, cut into 3" pieces	2 T. chopped green bell pepper
2 lg. onions, coarsely chopped	1 T. dry mustard
2 c. canned tomato sauce	4 lg. garlic cloves, minced
4 lg. jalapeño chilies, finely chopped (about 1/4 c.)	1/2 tsp. cayenne pepper
	1/4 tsp. ground cloves
1/4 c. red wine vinegar	1/4 tsp. cinnamon
1/4 c. firmly-packed golden brown sugar	2 c. beer ☺
	Minced fresh cilantro or parsley

Preheat oven to 425°. Arrange short ribs in single layer in 2 large baking pans. Sprinkle onions around ribs. Combine all remaining ingredients, except beer and cilantro, in large saucepan. Simmer over medium heat until slightly thickened, stirring occasionally, about 10 minutes. Cool slightly. Stir in beer. Pour mixture over ribs. Cover pans with foil and bake until meat is very tender, 2 1/2 hours.

Remove ribs from pan and keep warm. Combine all pan juices in heavy medium saucepan. Skim fat from pan juices. Boil over medium heat until liquid is reduced to 2 cups, if necessary. Spoon sauce over ribs. (Can be prepared 1 day ahead. Return ribs and sauce to pans. Cover and refrigerate. Remove any hardened fat from surface. Cover pans with foil. Bake in 375° oven until meat is heated through, about 45 minutes.) Sprinkle with cilantro and serve.

"1st and 10" Shisk K-Bobs

4 to 6 servings

3 lb. meat (1" thick)
1/2 c. salad oil
1/2 c. beer or ale ☺
1/4 c. vinegar
1/4 c. brown sugar
2 T. soy sauce
1 clove garlic, crushed
1 tsp. dried parsley
1/4 tsp. dry mustard

1/4 tsp. crushed basil
1/4 tsp. Tabasco sauce
6 to 8 sm. white onions
6 to 8 mushrooms
1 green pepper, sliced into 2"
   pieces
2 firm tomatoes, cut in wedges
1 c. (8 oz. can) tomato sauce

Cut meat in 2-inch pieces, removing any gristle and most of fat. To make marinade, combine next 10 ingredients in bowl. Add meat and let stand, in bowl or recloseable plastic bag, in refrigerator at least 3 hours, or overnight. Turn occasionally.

When ready to cook, peel onions and remove stems from mushrooms. Alternate marinated meat with vegetables on 6-inch metal skewers. Add tomato sauce to remaining marinade to make barbecue sauce; brush over vegetables and meat. Broil over coals or in oven broiler 3 inches from heat source until meat is tender, about 15 minutes. Brush frequently with sauce and turn skewers to brown kebobs.

Until I was thirteen, I thought my name was SHUT UP.
--Joe Namath

Beef 'n Brew Kabobs

6 servings

1 c. beer ☺
3/4 c. steak sauce
2 cloves garlic, crushed
2 tsp. chili powder
1 tsp. ground cumin

1 1/2 lb. round steaks, cut into 1/2"
  strips
3 sm. red or green peppers, cut
  into 1" pieces
1 tsp. cornstarch

Blend beer, steak sauce, garlic, chili powder and cumin in non-metal dish. Pour the marinade over sliced steak. Cover and chill about 2 hours, stirring occasionally. Remove steak from marinade, but do not discard marinade. Thread steak and pepper pieces on 6 skewers. Heat remaining marinade and cornstarch. Bring to a boil. Grill or broil kabobs 4 inches from heat for 15 minutes, or until done, turning and brushing with marinade often.

When we drink, we get drunk. When we get drunk, we fall asleep.
When we fall asleep, we commit no sin. When we commit no sin, we go to heaven.
Soooo, let's all get drunk and go to heaven!
                          --Brian O'Rourke

Lacrosse Onion Burgers

8 oz. ground beef
1/4 c. beer ☺
1 tsp. seasoned salt
2 Kaiser rolls, split
2 T. butter

1 sm. onion, sliced & separated in
   rings
1 T. steak sauce
1/4 tsp. dried leaf basil
1/4 tsp. dried leaf thyme
Lettuce & tomato slices (opt.)

In medium bowl, mix beef, 1/4 cup beer and seasoned salt. Shape into 2 patties. Cook patties in medium skillet over medium heat about 15 minutes, until done as desired, turning frequently. Place on bottom half of rolls.

Rugby Bar-B-Qued Beef

4 lb. ground beef
2 lg. onions, minced
1 T. salt
1 tsp. pepper
1/3 c. all-purpose flour

1 qt. flat beer ☺
1 T. Worcestershire sauce
3 c. ketchup
1 to 2 T. chili powder
30 to 32 buns

Cook beef in 2 pans, stirring to keep crumbly, until it looses red color. Add onions and pepper and salt. Add flour; mix well. Slowly add water and rest of ingredients, except for the buns. Simmer, uncovered, for 20 minutes, stirring once or twice. Serve hot on toasted buns.
   Filling and buns can be prepared a day ahead and reheated to serve.

"Prize-Fightin" Bar-B-Que Meat Balls

SAUCE:
1 btl. catsup
1 btl. chili sauce
1/2 c. prepared mustard (can use hot mustard)
1 1/2 c. brown sugar
2 tsp. black pepper

1/4 c. lemon juice
1/2 c. steak sauce
1/3 to 1/2 c. Worcestershire sauce (use more to make it spicy)
1 T. soy sauce

MEAT BALLS:
1 c. beer ☺
Garlic salt
5 lb. hamburger

1 egg for each lb. of meat
2 pkg. crushed soda crackers

Roll meat in small balls and broil. Pour sauce over broiled meat balls and bake at 350° for 1 hour.

I don't feel old. I don't feel anything until noon. Then it's time for my nap.
--Bob Hope

Beer and Bacon Spaghetti Sauce

About 2 quarts

4 slices bacon
8 med. onions, chopped
2 cloves garlic, minced
1 1/2 lb. ground beef
1 c. grated Parmesan cheese
1 tsp. basil
2 T. Worcestershire sauce
1 (6 oz.) can sliced mushrooms

1 T. parsley flakes
1 (12 oz.) can beer ☺
1 (6 oz.) can tomato paste
1 tsp. salt
1/2 tsp. Tabasco sauce
1 1/2 tsp. oregano
1 (No. 1) can tomato purée

Fry bacon until crisp; drain. Remove bacon. To bacon fat in skillet, add onions and garlic; sauté until golden. Add ground beef and cheese; stir often. Cook until brown. Add beer; cook 10 minutes. Add tomato paste, salt, Tabasco sauce, Worcestershire sauce, oregano, basil and parsley, and simmer 10 minutes. Add tomato purée, mushrooms and bacon. Continue cooking until thickened, about 10 minutes.

"Par for the Course" Shredded Beef

Put in slow-cooker.

5 lb. chuck roast
3 cloves garlic, crushed
1 T. paprika
1 T. celery salt
1 T. garlic powder
1 T. dried parsley
1/2 T. ground black pepper
1/2 T. chili powder
1/2 T. cayenne pepper
1/2 tsp. seasoned salt

1/2 tsp. mustard powder
1/2 tsp. dried tarragon
4 oz. beer ☺
1 1/2 T. Worcestershire sauce
4 T. hot pepper sauce
2 tsp. liquid smoke flavoring
1 lg. onion, chopped
1 green bell pepper, chopped
2 jalapeño chili peppers, chopped

Using a sharp knife, poke several 1-inch deep holes in the roast. Insert the garlic slivers into the holes.

In a small bowl, combine the paprika, celery salt, garlic powder, parsley, ground black pepper, chili powder, cayenne pepper and seasoned salt. Mix together well and rub over the meat.

In a separate small bowl, combine the beer or cola, Worcestershire sauce, hot pepper sauce and liquid smoke, and mix well. Place the roast in a slow-cooker and pour this mixture over the meat. Add the onion, green bell pepper and jalapeño chili peppers to the slow-cooker. Cook on low setting for 10 hours, or more, if desired.

Serve with tortillas and also makes great sandwiches.

"Knock Out" Chili Con Carne

3 to 4 lb. ground chuck
1 lg. green pepper
1 med. onion
2 garlic cloves
Salad oil
1 tsp. crushed red pepper (more if you like spicy)
2 T. chili powder

1 1/4 tsp. cumin
1 can tomatoes
1 can tomato paste
1 can beer ☺
2 T. brown sugar
1 1/2 tsp. oregano
1 1/2 tsp. salt
2 cans red kidney beans

CHILI ACCOMPANIMENTS:
Shredded cheese
Sour cream

Chopped onion

In skillet, brown meat. Add chopped onion, pepper, garlic and crushed red pepper until tender. Stir in chili powder and cumin; cook 1 minute. Pour in large pot with lid. Add tomatoes with their liquid, tomato paste, beer, brown sugar, oregano and salt. Heat to boiling; reduce to low. Cover and simmer 45 minutes. Drain and rinse kidney beans. Add to mixture. Simmer 15 minutes.

Beauty lies in the hands of the beer holder.
--Anonymous

"World Series" Chili for Dogs

2 lb. ground beef
16 oz. tomato sauce
1 onion, diced
2 tsp. garlic powder
2 1/2 tsp. chili powder
2 tsp. oregano
2 tsp. salt
4 tsp. ground cumin

1/2 to 1 tsp. ground cayenne
   pepper
2 pkg. hot dogs, sliced in 1/2"
   segments
2 cans diced tomatoes
2 cans dark kidney beans
1 can beer ☺
Shredded cheese

Brown beef and onions. Add tomato sauce and garlic powder. Cover and simmer for 30 minutes. During the simmering, brown the hot dog slices in a pan. Add remaining ingredients and hot dogs. Stir, cover, and simmer for 1 hour. (Do not uncover to stir while simmering.) Top with shredded cheese and serve with crackers.

Never let the fear of striking out get in your way.
--George Herman "Babe" Ruth

"Double Play" Beer Chili

2 T. vegetable oil
3 onions, chopped
3 cloves garlic, minced
1 lb. ground beef
3/4 lb. beef sirloin, cubed
1 (14.5 oz.) can peeled & diced
  tomatoes with juice
1 btl. dark beer ☺
1 c. strong coffee
2 sm. cans tomato paste
1 (14 oz.) can beef broth

1/2 c. packed brown sugar
3 to 4 T. chili powder
1 T. cumin seeds
1 T. unsweetened cocoa powder
1 tsp. dried oregano
1 tsp. ground cayenne pepper
1 tsp. ground coriander
1 tsp. salt
4 fresh hot chili peppers, seeded &
  chopped
Kidney beans (opt.)

Heat oil in a large saucepan over medium heat. Cook onions, garlic, ground beef and cubed sirloin in oil for 10 minutes, or until the meat is well browned and the onions are tender. Stir in the diced tomatoes with juice, dark beer, coffee, tomato paste and beef broth. Season with brown sugar, chili powder, cumin, cocoa powder, oregano, cayenne pepper, coriander and salt. Stir in hot chili peppers. Reduce heat to low, and simmer for over an hour.

If you add beans, cook on low for another 30 minutes. I usually cook them separately because there is always someone who won't eat them.

Serve with grated Cheddar cheese and onions.

"Lineman" Beef Goulash

4 to 6 servings

2 to 3 lb. chuck steak, cut into
  1 1/2" pieces
1 T. flour
1 tsp. salt
Pepper
2 tsp. paprika
1/4 c. salad oil
2 cloves garlic, chopped
1 bay leaf
1/4 tsp. ground coriander

1 (12 oz.) can beer (1 1/2 c.) ☺
1 (10 1/2 oz.) can beef broth
3 onions, chopped (use 2 if onions
  are lg.)
3 carrots, sliced crosswise
4 med. potatoes, quartered
4 tomatoes, peeled & cut into sm.
  pieces
1 tsp. caraway seeds

  Mix flour, salt, pepper and paprika together and toss meat in it. Heat oil, add meat and garlic and fry until well browned. Add bay leaf, coriander, beer and beef broth; stir until boiling, then transfer all to a 3-quart casserole. Cover and cook in 350° oven for 2 hours. Add onions, carrots, potatoes, tomatoes and caraway seeds; continue cooking for another hour. Taste and adjust seasonings.

May your glass be ever full. May the roof over your head be always strong.
And may you be in the heaven half an hour before the devil knows you're dead.
--Old Irish Toast

Veal

Stuffed Veal

6 servings

1 sm. onion, minced	2 lb. veal steak, cut in very thin
2 T. butter, melted	slices
3 c. soft bread crumbs	Seasoned flour
2 T. water	2 T. fat or salad oil
1/2 tsp. salt	1 bay leaf
Few grains pepper	1 onion, sliced
1 tsp. poultry seasoning	1 (6 oz.) can tomato sauce
	1 1/2 c. any beer ☺

Combine minced onion, melted butter, crumbs, water, salt, pepper and poultry seasoning to make stuffing; mix well. Spread on veal slices. Roll up each slice, fasten with toothpicks. Roll in seasoned flour; brown in hot fat or salad oil. Add bay leaf and sliced onion. Combine tomato sauce and beer; pour over all. Cover; simmer 1 hour, or until tender. Thicken gravy, if desired.

Lamb

Leg of Lamb

2 to 3 lb. leg of lamb
1 pt. dark beer or ale ☺
2 to 3 onions, sliced thin

Salt & pepper, to taste
2 T. butter
1/2 tsp. cider vinegar (opt.)

Trim fat and bone the lamb. Cut meat across grain into thin slices. Put in heavy pan with a lid. Add onion and simmer for half hour, or until tender. Add vinegar, if desired.

By the time a man is wise enough to watch his step, he's too old to go anywhere.
--Billy Crystal

Lamb with Sour Cream and Capers

2 to 3 servings

Makes a great sauce.

2 or 3 lamb shanks, divided into 3 pieces each
2 T. vegetable oil
1 tsp. salt
3/4 to 1 c. beer ☺

In cheesecloth, add bay leaf & 2 sprigs parsley & thyme (better if fresh; can use dried herbs, but add more to taste)
1/2 to 3/4 c. sour cream
2 or 3 T. capers

Brown shanks in oil or drippings in a Dutch oven or heavy pot with a lid. Add some salt, beer and garni (cheesecloth with spices tied in it and then tie a string on handle of pot). Cover and cook, turning a few times, on top of stove, or can put in oven at 300° for 1 1/2 to 2 hours. Remove lamb to a bowl or deep platter. Skim off fat. Mix sour cream and capers into pot. Stir and pour over lamb.
Yum!

Golf's a hard game to figure. One day you'll go out and
slice it and shank it, hit into all the traps and miss every green.
The next day you go out and for no reason at all you really stink.
--Anonymous

Game

Venison Stir-Fry

2 lb. venison or beef steak, cut
  across grain into 1/4" strips
2 T. beer ☺
2 T. soy sauce
1 T. cornstarch
1/4 tsp. black pepper
1/4 tsp. powdered ginger
1/4 tsp. garlic powder

2 T. oil
2 (6 oz.) pkg. frozen pea pods
1 c. sliced fresh mushrooms, or
  1 (8 oz.) can sliced mushrooms
1 c. thin-sliced carrots
1/2 to 1 c. thin-sliced onions
1 (6 oz.) can sliced water chestnuts

Place meat in shallow pan. In small bowl, combine wine, soy sauce, cornstarch, pepper, ginger, garlic powder. Pour over meat. Marinate 1 hour at room temperature or in refrigerator overnight.

When ready to cook, pour oil in wok and preheat to 375°. Drain meat, reserve marinade. Place half of meat in hot oil and stir-fry for 3 minutes, or until brown. Remove and add remaining meat and brown. Add onions and fry for 3 minutes. Push up side or remove. Add carrots and fry for 3 minutes. Add pea pods and fry until completely thawed. Add mushrooms and fry for 1 to 2 minutes. Add sliced chestnuts and fry for 1 minute.

Return all fried ingredients to wok and add remaining marinade. Stir gently to combine all ingredients. Reduce heat to simmer. Simmer for 4 to 5 minutes, or until heated through.

Serve with rice or noodles.

Braised Rabbit or Chicken in Beer

4 servings

I can picture a bunch of guys on a hunting trip drinking beer and cooking rabbit. Go for it. Me--I don't eat Bambi (venison), Big Bird (ostrich) or The Easter Bunny (rabbit). Most women would gag at the thought of this but I decided to include it for the He-Man types!

1 cut-up fryer	1/4 c. chili sauce
2 T. cooking oil	1 T. brown sugar
3 cut-up potatoes	1 clove minced garlic
4 cut carrots	1/3 c. cold water
1 thin-sliced onion	3 T. flour
1 c. beer ☺	1/2 tsp. salt

Brown meat in hot oil; drain. In crockery cooker, place potatoes, carrots and onion; put meat on top. Combine chili sauce, beer, brown sugar and garlic. Pour over meat. Cover, cook on high for 4 to 5 hours. Remove meat, drain vegetables, reserve liquid. Measure liquid; add beer or water if needed to measure 1 1/2 cups.

In saucepan, blend cold water into flour, stir in reserved liquid (salt). Cook until thickened. Place meat and vegetables on a platter, garnish with parsley, pass the gravy.

Reality is an illusion that occurs due to the lack of alcohol.
--Anonymous

Pork

"Atlanta-Style Ribs"

The peaches add a great flavor!

1 beer (not dark or lite) ☺
1 btl. Pete's barbecue sauce

1 can canned or very ripe peaches, smashed

In a large pot, cover ribs with cold water and a can of beer. Bring to boil and reduce heat to a simmer. Simmer for about 30 minutes. Rinse and drain.

Combine barbecue sauce and smashed peaches and coat ribs on all sides. Put in refrigerator to marinate for up to 8 hours.

Cook on grill at least 6 inches away from heat, basting frequently with sauce until done.

Abstainer: A weak person who yields to the
temptation of denying himself a pleasure.
--Ambrose Bierce

This Little Piggy Went to Market Stew

4 to 6 servings

2 T. salad oil
2 lb. lean pork shoulder, cut into
  bite-size cubes
Salt & freshly-ground pepper
2 c. beer ☺
2 c. beef broth
1 tsp. dried rosemary

10 sm. white onions, peeled (can
  leave whole or cut in half)
3 med. potatoes, peeled &
  quartered
4 carrots, scraped & cut in half
Instant blending flour

Heat the oil in a Dutch oven, and brown the pork on all sides. Season with salt and pepper. Add the beer and 1/4 cup of the beef broth, and the rosemary; cover and simmer slowly for 1 to 1 1/2 hours. During the cooking time, baste or turn the meat so the pork can really stew. If the liquid is reducing too quickly, add a little more broth or beer. Add the onions, potatoes, carrots, and a cup of the broth. Stir all the ingredients and simmer, covered, for 30 minutes. Gradually add some instant blending flour to the stew and cook, stirring constantly, until the sauce thickens.

WARNING: The consumption of alcohol may make you think you have mystical Kung Fu powers, resulting in you getting your butt kicked.
--Anonymous

Quick and Easy Pork Stew with Fruit

2 T. oil
1 med. onion, chopped
1 1/2 to 2 lb. pork, cut in bite-size
  cubes
1/4 tsp. oregano
1 clove garlic, chopped
1 tsp. cinnamon
1 tsp. brown sugar

1/4 tsp. salt
1/2 tsp. pepper
1 (12 oz.) can beer☺
15 prunes
1 can sweet potatoes, drained (if
  you use fresh, cook first)
2 T. cornstarch
Water (add until smooth)

Put oil in pot and sauté onion and pork for 7 minutes. Add next 8 ingredients; bring to boil. Cover and simmer for 10 to 15 minutes. Take cover off and add sweet potatoes. Thicken with cornstarch and water, and heat for 2 minutes.

A "gimme" can best be defined as an agreement between two golfers..
neither of whom can putt very well.
--Anonymous

"Three Pointer" Grilled Pork Roast

Need to marinate for 6 to 8 hours. So do this the night before or the morning the day you wish to serve.

3 to 4 lb. boneless pork loin roast	1 (12 oz.) can (1 1/2 c.) beer ☺
2 T. Worcestershire sauce	1 T. dried minced onion
1 tsp. dry mustard	2 T. brown sugar
1/2 tsp. salt	

Mix ingredients, except brown sugar. Place in plastic bag with meat. Refrigerate 6 hours, or overnight, turning occasionally. Drain meat and save marinade. Put meat thermometer in center of roast. Stir brown sugar in marinade. In a covered grill, arrange preheated coals around a drip pan. Place roast over drip pan but not over coals. Close grill. Grill about 1 1/2 to 2 hours, or until thermometer registers 170°. Brush with marinade every 15 minutes.

Tastes great with Hot German Potato Salad.

It's better to have beer in hand than gas in tank.
--Anonymous

Honey Grilled Pork

This recipe only requires 1 hour to marinate. If you like to do get-togethers at the last minute, this works and tastes great.

3 to 5 lb. boneless pork loin roast	**1 c. beer** ☺
1/2 c. honey	**1/2 c. Dijon mustard**
1/4 c. vegetable oil	**2 T. onion powder**
1 1/2 tsp. rosemary leaves, crushed	**1 tsp. salt**
1/4 tsp. black pepper	**1 tsp. garlic powder**

Place pork in heavy plastic bag. Combine remaining ingredients; pour over pork. Seal bag. Marinate in refrigerator 1 hour. Remove pork from marinade. Place over drip pan filled with 1 inch of water on grill. Grill, uncovered, or bake at 350° for 30 minutes per pound, or until 160° internal temperature, basting occasionally. Simmer any leftover marinade 5 minutes. Serve with roast.

With a larger roast, you may want to adjust the amount of honey and other seasonings.

If you ever reach total enlightenment while drinking beer,
I bet it makes beer shoot out your nose.
--Deep Thought, Jack Handy

Brainless Ham on the Grill

It is really tough to screw this up!

1 (5 lb.) can canned ham

Use beer opener and make a hole on each end or side of ham and put on the grill. When the gel turns to liquid (about 15 minutes), pour it out. Then make holes every 2 inches around the top of canned ham and pour in the rest.

1/2 c. maple syrup	**3 tsp. chili powder**
1/2 c. beer ☺	**1 tsp. celery**

Cook on grill for 1 1/2 hours. May need to add more beer if it evaporates too quickly, or lower heat source a few inches.

WARNING: The consumption of alcohol may cause a disturbance in the time-space continuum, whereby small (and sometimes large) gaps of time may seem to literally disappear.
--Anonymous

Marinated Brats

6 servings

Make marinade ahead.

6 brats	**1 T. prepared mustard**
1 (12 oz.) can beer (or bottle) ☺	**1 tsp. chili powder**
2 T. brown sugar	**2 cloves garlic, minced**
2 T. soy sauce	**Several drops hot pepper sauce**

Combine beer, brown sugar, soy sauce, mustard, chili powder, garlic and hot pepper sauce. Place brats in shallow baking dish; pour marinade over. Cover, refrigerate several hours, or overnight, spooning marinade occasionally. Remove brats, reserve marinade. Grill over medium-hot coals about 4 minutes. Turn and grill until done, about 3 to 4 minutes more.

Always do sober what you said you'd do drunk.
That will teach you to keep your mouth shut.
--Ernest Hemingway

"Full House" Brats 'n Buns

2 to 3 beers ☺
6, 12 or 24 brats & buns
  (depending on number of
  guests)
1, 2 or 3 onions

Green, red, yellow peppers
Spicy mustard
Warm sauerkraut, for topping
  (opt.)

Fill a large pot with beer and add water. Bring to a boil and cook brats for about 5 minutes. Haul pot and brats to grill (or if you are lucky enough to have a burner right next to your grill, use it). Throw all the brats on grill and brown. Then put brats back in beer pot to keep moist until ready to serve. Sauté onions and peppers for topping.

Serve with corn on the cob, potato salad, sliced tomatoes and plenty of cold beer.

WARNING: The consumption of alcohol may make
you think you are whispering when you are not.
                   --Anonymous

Polish Sausage with Cabbage and Apples

6 servings

(You can also use smoked sausage or brats.)
Great one-dish meal!

4 T. bacon fat
2 T. sugar
2 sm. yellow onions, chopped (or 1 lg.)
6 c. shredded red cabbage
2 tart red apples, such as Jonathan, cored & slice thin but not peeled
2 T. cider vinegar

1/2 tsp. caraway seeds
1 1/2 lb. Polish-style smoked sausage links, or bratwursts
1 lb. new potatoes
Salt & freshly-ground black pepper, to taste
1 c. beer (any kind) ☺

Melt the bacon fat in a large skillet over medium heat. Add the sugar and cook, stirring often, until the sugar browns, about 4 minutes. Reduce the heat to medium-low, add the onion and sauté it until it is golden, about 5 minutes. Add the cabbage, apples, vinegar and caraway seeds; stir to blend.

Place the sausage links and the potatoes on top of the cabbage mixture. Season with salt and pepper and pour the beer over all. Bring the mixture to a boil over medium-high heat, reduce the heat and simmer, covered, for 45 minutes.

Adjust the seasonings to your taste. I like to add another apple, a tad more sugar, and a little more cider.

Brats 'n Sauce

6 grilled brats
5 or 6 sliced onions
1 c. chili sauce
1 T. Worcestershire sauce
1 c. ketchup

2 T. vinegar
1/2 tsp. salt
2 T. brown sugar
1 tsp. paprika
1 beer ☺

In a large pot, add all ingredients and cook for about 1/2 hour. Add grilled brats.

This is great for leftover brats, or you can pre-grill them and throw them into the sauce.

A man boards a bus after a game of golf. He has several golf balls in his pockets. He sits down next to a blonde and she sits quietly but her eyes can't avoid his pockets.

He said, "I have golf balls."

She thought quietly and finally said, "Does it hurt as bad as tennis elbow?"

Ribs and Beer

Make marinade 4 to 6 hours ahead.

1/3 c. dark beer ☺
1/3 c. soy sauce
1/3 c. Dijon mustard
4 lb. spareribs

1 med. onion, minced
1 tsp. Worcestershire sauce
1/4 c. dark brown sugar, firmly
   packed

In a large bowl, combine everything but ribs to form a marinade. In a kettle, cover spareribs with cold water. Bring to a boil, reduce heat to just simmering. Simmer 35 to 40 minutes. Drain and rinse with cold water. Add ribs to marinade and toss to coat. Marinate 4 hours (or longer) at room temperature, or overnight in the refrigerator, turning occasionally.

Cook on grill about 6 to 7 inches from heat. Baste every 15 minutes or so. You can cut the ribs into individual ribs and serve as appetizers.

An interesting thing about golf is that no matter how badly you play;
it is always possible to get worse.
                    --Anonymous

Bon Bon's Babyback Ribs

Prepare in the morning, throw in oven, and cook all day.

This is another one of my brainless, fail-safe recipes. Works great when you have a busy day and family or guest's are showing up for dinner, or you just want to go shopping.

3 to 4 big meaty slab of ribs	**Salt & pepper**
2 (28 oz.) btl. Bulls-Eye barbecue	**1 or 2 cans or btl. beer ☺**
sauce	

Rinse ribs and cut any additional fat off them. Put in a self-basting large turkey roaster pan. Add beer and enough water to just cover ribs. Salt and pepper ribs. Put lid on and throw in oven at 225° to 250° and cook all day.

Make sure lid is on right to allow ribs to cook with steam. Drain fat from ribs. Throw bottles of sauce on last 3 or 4 hours. Serve.

I also wrap bake potatoes in foil and throw them in the oven all day too. Then you can serve slaw, beans, corn on the cob, or whatever at the last minute.

"Giddy-Up 409" Ribs

8 to 12 servings (depends on size of ribs)

3 c. beer ☺
2 c. packed dark brown sugar
1/4 c. cider vinegar
1 T. chili powder
2 tsp. ground cumin
2 tsp. dry mustard
1/2 tsp. red pepper
1/2 tsp. ground cloves

4 cloves garlic, peeled & crushed
1 bay leaf
8 slabs trimmed pork baby back
   ribs (about 2 lb. each)
Salt
Lawry's seasoning (can use Mrs.
   Dash or Accent)

   Combine beef, brown sugar, vinegar, chili powder, ground cumin, dry mustard, ground cloves, garlic and bay leaf in a large bowl; stir until thoroughly blended. Place ribs in 2 or 3 large roasting pans, pour marinade evenly over ribs; turn ribs to coat. Marinate ribs, covered, in refrigerator 24 hours, turning and basting often.

   Heat oven to 350°. Lift ribs from marinade, draining excess marinade back into pans. Combine marinade from all pans in bowl, reserve. Rinse out the roasting pans; line pans with heavy-duty aluminum foil. Place 3 slabs of ribs in single layer in each roasting pan. Sprinkle generously with salt and seasoning. Roast ribs, basting often with half of reserved marinade, until ribs are evenly browned and crisp on both sides, about 1 1/2 hours. Turn ribs and rotate pans occasionally. When ribs are cooked, transfer to heatproof platter; cover with foil and keep warm.

Chinese-Style Ribs

3/4 c. beer ☺
1/3 c. hoisin sauce
1/3 c. soy sauce
1/3 c. honey
1/3 c. thin-sliced scallions

1 tsp. ground ginger
2 T. minced fresh garlic
1 T. cider vinegar
6 lb. pork spareribs

In a small saucepan, mix beer, hoisin, soy sauce, honey, scallions, ginger, garlic and vinegar. Bring to a boil over medium heat. Reduce heat and simmer, uncovered, for 5 minutes. Remove from heat; cool to room temperature.

Place ribs in a shallow, non-metal pan large enough to hold them in one layer. Pour marinade over ribs, cover and let stand to marinate at least 1 hour, turning once.

Heat oven to 475°. Transfer ribs to a rack in a roasting pan large enough to hold ribs in one layer. Reserve marinade. Bake 20 minutes. Reduce heat to 300°. Bake 1 to 1 1/4 hours, turning twice and basting with marinade during the last 30 minutes, until ribs are tender when pierced with a fork.

Confused Grill

(AKA - Mixed Grill)

1 or 2 slabs pork spareribs (split in half)
2 chickens, cut up
1 c. soy sauce
1 sm. can pineapple, with juice
1 c. brown sugar
3 T. ground allspice

1 T. ground thyme
2 T. ground mustard
1 clove crushed garlic
1/3 c. crushed fresh ginger, or season to taste
1/2 c. beer ☺

Place meat in large marinating pan. Add the ingredients in any order. Soak (marinate) for 3 hours or more. Start the grill; when charcoals are gray, place meat on grill. Do not burn the meat, but let it get crispy and keep turning until cooked.

WARNING: The consumption of alcohol may lead you to believe that ex-lovers are really dying for you to telephone them at four in the morning.
--Anonymous

Happy Honey Garlic Ribs

Place the racks of ribs on the foil-lined rack of your oven, turning frequently for about 45 minutes. Baste several times with beer ☺, water or chicken broth, and remove fat as it accumulates in the foil trough. At the end of 45 minutes, remove foil from rack. Continue cooking the ribs on the bare rack until they are cooked through, about 45 minutes more. Keep turning and basting with beer ☺, water or broth. The outside of the ribs should be the color of dark mahogany.

Transfer ribs to cutting board and cut into individual ribs. Brush with sauce. Return to rack; turn ribs and brush second side and edges with sauce. Continue to cook, turning often and brushing with more sauce until ribs are well glazed, about 15 minutes longer. Serve immediately.

HONEY GARLIC SAUCE:

1/2 c. honey	**3 tsp. tomato catsup**
1/2 c. soy sauce	**1/2 c. water**
2 cloves garlic, crushed	

Make a marinade with above ingredients. Allow the ribs to stand in this for several hours, turning a few times. Cook for 1 to 1 1/2 hours, basting occasionally, until the ribs are shiny brown and tender to the fork.

Sloppy Barb-Q Ribs

Ribs (as many as you want)
Beer (enough to pour over ribs) ☺
Salt & pepper, to taste
Marjoram, sprinkled generously
1 btl. hickory smoke barbecue
  sauce

1 tsp. prepared mustard
1/4 c. vinegar
3 T. brown sugar
1/8 tsp. garlic powder
1 (8 oz.) can tomato sauce
2 tsp. crushed red pepper

Don't separate ribs, soak them overnight in beer in oven pan. Next day, salt and pepper to taste. Sprinkle marjoram all over the ribs. Rub into ribs. Brown ribs on grill on both sides to give a crust. Then sprinkle with beer and cook 1 to 1 1/2 hours. Cut into individual ribs. Slop both sides with sauce.

Sauce: Combine last 7 ingredients and cook sauce until it simmers; keep warm.

Ribs for 2

1 rack of ribs
4 T. molasses
3 T. vinegar or lemon juice
4 T. prepared mustard

2 T. steak sauce
2 T. Tabasco sauce
1 can beer (may be non-
  alcoholic) ☺

Combine all ingredients. Pour or brush on ribs. Save some of the sauce to use for basting. Bake at 375° for about 1 1/2 hours.

Rag Apple Ribs

SAUCE:

2 T. olive oil

1 med. chopped onion

1 (8 oz.) can tomato sauce

1/2 c. brown sugar

1/4 c. white sugar

1 tsp. Worcestershire sauce

2 T. chili powder

1/2 tsp. dry mustard

Pinch of salt

RIBS:

6 to 8 lb. ribs

2 Granny Smith apples

12 oz. beer ☺

3 to 4 chopped garlic cloves

Sauce: Combine all ingredients in saucepan. Bring to a boil, stirring occasionally. Reduce heat and simmer 30 to 45 minutes.

Ribs: Place ribs in a large pot with whole apples, vinegar, beer and garlic. Fill pot with water, cover and bring to a boil. Skim fat. Reduce heat to a simmer and cook 45 minutes. Meat should be almost ready to fall off of bones. Baste ribs with sauce and grill over charcoal, turning several times.

I drink to make other people interesting.
--George Jean Nathan

"He-Man" Country-Style Ribs

(These are the bigger, meatier ribs, not spareribs.)

4 lb. country-style pork ribs

POACHING LIQUID:

1 (12 oz.) btl. beer (1 1/2 c.) ☺
1/2 c. tomato juice
1/4 c. lemon juice

Dash of cayenne pepper
4 whole cloves
1 lg. onion, quartered

SKEWERS:

1 fresh pineapple, pared, cored &
  cut into chunks

Select meaty ribs with a minimum of bones. Combine beer, tomato juice, lemon juice, cayenne, cloves and onions in large bowl. Add the ribs; simmer, covered, for 30 minutes. Drain. Place pineapple chunks on skewers. Preheat charcoal or broiler.

BASTING SAUCE:

1/2 c. honey
1/2 c. soy sauce
1/4 c. chili sauce

1/4 c. red wine vinegar
1/4 tsp. Worcestershire sauce
1 clove garlic, minced or mashed

Continued on following page.

Continued from preceding page.

Basting Sauce: Combine honey, soy sauce, chili sauce and garlic, vinegar and Worcestershire sauce.

Grill meat and the skewers, brushing often with the basting sauce until glazed and shiny, about 15 minutes. Turn both meat and skewers over during grilling time.

Ribs can be precooked the day before.

Grill about 15 minutes.

All right, brain, I don't like you and you don't like me,
so let's just do this and I'll get back to killing you with beer.
--Homer Simpson

Slathered Mesquite-Smoked Ribs

Make 1 day ahead for rub.

3 slabs baby back ribs
Rib rub (your favorite)
6 or 12 pack beer ☺
Mesquite chips
2 cloves garlic, minced
4 T. olive oil
1 c. onion, chopped
1 1/3 c. cider vinegar
1/2 c. brown sugar

2 (about 16 oz.) cans tomato sauce
Hot sauce
Salt
Fresh pepper
1 T. Worcestershire sauce
Yellow mustard
Dash of cayenne pepper
2 sweet onions
2 green peppers

Sauce: Heat olive oil in a medium saucepan on medium heat. Sauté onion and garlic 2 or 3 minutes. Add the vinegar and cook for 3 minutes. Add remaining ingredients, and bring to a low boil; reduce to a simmer for 1 hour. Cool, then serve or refrigerate.

Depending on the amount of "kick" you like, adjust the amount of salt (approximately 2 teaspoons), hot sauce (approximately 3 teaspoons), mustard (3 or 4 good squirts) and cayenne (a few dashes).

One day ahead, liberally rub the ribs with your favorite rub (store-bought or homemade). Wrap each piece tightly in plastic wrap, and then in aluminum foil. Refrigerate for 1 day.

Continued on following page.

Continued from preceding page.

Soak chips in water for about 30 minutes, then dry. Heat one side of the grill, and add the chips. When they start smoking, add the ribs, cut in half slabs, to the opposite side of the grill, preferably on a top rack. Pour 1 can beer into a disposable aluminum pan, and place over the heat at the back of the grill (this will create moisture inside to self-baste ribs). Cook on a low heat. Use a grill thermometer to ensure a temperature of 200° to 225°. Close the lid to allow the ribs to soak the smoke flavor up, but monitor the temperature, and add chips as needed, to keep the smoke billowing.

Every 15 minutes or so, baste the ribs. You can use a mix of cider vinegar, lemon juice, hot sauce, pepper, Worcestershire sauce and a little mustard for this. When the ribs are close to being done, but not quite, pull them. Rib cook times vary - at this temperature about 3 to 4 hours would be a good time to check.

When the meat has cooked down from the bone, and the ribs sag on the ends when picked up in the middle by tongs, remove them from the grill.

Preheat the oven to 200°. Cut into slices sweet onion and green pepper. Place these into the bottom of a baking pan. Cover with beer and water. Slather the ribs with BBQ sauce, then place into the pan. Seal tight with aluminum foil and bake for 1 to 1 1/2 hours.

Good smoked ribs require tender loving care, and while not overly difficult, are time consuming.

Golf is a game of expletives - not deleted.
--Dr. Irving A. Gladstone

166

"Go Golfin" Beer BBQ Ribs

You can fit in at least 9 holes while these bake!

4 lb. boneless country-style pork **4 oz. hickory smoke flavoring**
 ribs (12 oz. per person) **1 beer** ☺

BARBECUE SAUCE:
8 c. barbecue sauce (your favorite) **1 c. beer** ☺
8 c. honey Dijon dressing

Layer ribs into pan; fill with water to 1 inch above ribs. Add hickory flavoring and beer. Bring to a boil. Reduce heat to a simmer; cook 25 to 35 minutes, until ribs are fully cooked. While ribs are simmering, mix together barbecue sauce ingredients. Drain water off the ribs, then place in foil-lined baking pan. Fully cover ribs with barbecue sauce. Cover pan with foil and bake in 275° oven for 2 1/2 to 3 1/2 hours to produce slow-cooked tender ribs.

I've had a good day at golf when I don't fall out of the cart.
--Buddy Hackett

Teriyaki Pork Chops

6 servings

After being tenderized by a beer marinade, these chops require only a quick turn on the grill or under the broiler to form the centerpiece of a hearty meal.

1 c. teriyaki marinade
2 T. chopped fresh ginger root

2/3 c. beer (not dark) ☺
6 (1" thick) rib or loin pork chops

In a saucepan, combine the teriyaki marinade, the ginger root and the beer. Simmer the mixture until it is reduced to about 1 1/3 cups, and let the marinade cool until it is room temperature.

In a shallow baking dish large enough to hold the pork chops in one layer, combine the pork chops and the marinade, turning the chops to coat them thoroughly, and let the chops marinate, covered and chilled, turning them several times, overnight.

Pour the marinade into a saucepan and boil it for 5 minutes.

Grill the pork chops on an oiled rack set about 4 inches over glowing coals, basting them with the marinade during the last 5 minutes of the cooking time, for 8 minutes on each side, or until they are just cooked through.

Alternatively the pork chops may be broiled on the rack of a broiler pan under a preheated broiler in the same manner.

"Shoot Some Hoops"
Bar-B-Cued Pork Chops

You've got time to show up for a game.

**1 of your favorite btl. barbecue
  sauce
1/2 c. onion, chopped very fine
1/2 c. brown sugar
1/2 c. beer, for sauce ☺**

**2 cans beer, for chops ☺
1 tsp. lemon juice
1 tsp. Worcestershire sauce
Approx. 8 to 10 pork chops**

Mix all of the above ingredients together, except 2 cans beer and pork chops. Let simmer. Cook pork chops on grill and pour beer over them while cooking. When they're cooked through, put them in sauce mixture and simmer for as long as possible, at least 2 hours.

*The problem is not aiming too high in life and failing,
it is aiming too low and achieving.*
--Author Unknown

Notes & Recipes

Breads

FAVORITE RECIPES
FROM MY COOKBOOK

Recipe Name	Page Number

Breads

"Morning After Breakfast"
Bourbon, Beer and Sweet Potato Waffles

6 servings

1 1/2 c. flour	1 c. mashed cooked sweet
1 T. baking powder	potatoes, cooled (can also use
1/2 tsp. salt	canned yams, drained)
3 eggs, separated	2 T. melted butter
1/2 c. milk	Pinch of nutmeg
1/2 c. Stout ☺	Pinch of cardamom
2 T. bourbon ☺	Pinch of ginger

   Sift together flour, baking powder and salt. Beat the egg yolks and mix them with the milk, Stout, bourbon, sweet potatoes, melted butter and spices. Beat the egg whites until they form soft peaks and fold them into the batter. Pour into waffle iron and cook until lightly browned. Pour on plenty of maple syrup.

Beer: It's not just for breakfast anymore.
--Anonymous

"Batter Up" Buttermilk Beer Pancakes

4 servings

3 c. buttermilk pancake mix
2 T. vegetable oil
2 lg. eggs

1/4 can beer (your choice) ☺
Some milk

Put pancake mix in large bowl and add oil, eggs and beer. Add enough milk so that when you mix the batter with a whisk it becomes thin enough to pour (but not too thin). Be sure all lumps are gone. Pour desired-size pancakes on preheated (medium-high) griddle. Cook until light brown on both sides and cooked inside.

Catcher's Favorite Beer Batter Pancakes

2 c. biscuit mix
2 T. sugar
1/2 tsp. ground cinnamon
Dash of ground nutmeg

5 beaten eggs
1/2 c. beer ☺
2 T. cooking oil

In large mixing bowl, stir together the biscuit mix, sugar, ground cinnamon and ground nutmeg. Stir together the beaten eggs, beer and cooking oil. Add dry ingredients, stirring just until moistened. If lumpy, add a little more beer. Pour in frying pan and cook until slightly browned. Top with butter and syrup.

Sweet Beer Bread with Raisins

3 c. self-rising flour
3 eggs
1 can beer ☺

5 T. sugar
Raisins, a good handful

Blend and put half of dough into a well-greased loaf pan. Put cinnamon and brown sugar over the dough, add remaining dough. Let set in pan for about 10 minutes. Bake in a 350° oven for 1 hour. Sprinkle cinnamon and sugar on top of loaf. Cool on rack.

Corn Fritters in Beer Batter
(Yum!)

3/4 c. unsifted flour
1 lg. pinch of salt
2 eggs, separated
2 T. olive oil
1/4 c. warm beer (could be leftover
 from last night) ☺

Vegetable oil, for frying
Corn (peaches, strawberries,
 bananas or apples may be
 substituted)

Heat vegetable oil in a wok or deep pan until very hot. In a bowl, mix flour, salt and egg yolks; add olive oil and whip with whisk. Heat beer, mix into above mixture slowly. Mix thoroughly. Chill batter.
  Whip egg whites until stiff, fold into chilled batter. Dip corn or fruit into batter and deep-fry, turning only once. Sprinkle with confectioners' sugar before serving.

Stud Muffins

3 c. Bisquick mix
1 heaping T. sugar

1 egg, beaten
12 oz. beer ☺

Combine sugar and Bisquick. Add egg and beer. Put in greased muffin tins. Bake at 400° for 10 minutes, turn down to 350° for 10 minutes.

Hungry Man Beer Biscuits

2 c. biscuit mix
1/2 c. Cheddar cheese, grated

1/2 c. beer ☺

Blend all ingredients. Knead 5 times on floured board. Roll into a rectangle, 4 inches wide and 1/2 inch thick. Cut into about 8 triangles. Bake 8 to 10 minutes at 450°. Cool on wire rack.

Beer Cheese Bread

(Need Bread Machine)

1 pkg. active dry yeast
3 c. bread flour
1 T. sugar
1 1/2 tsp. salt
1 T. butter

10 oz. beer, room temp. ☺
4 oz. shredded or diced processed
   American cheese
4 oz. shredded or diced Monterey
   Jack cheese

On stove-top or in microwave, heat beer and American cheese together until just warm. There is no need to completely melt cheese. Stir; transfer mixture to bread machine pan. Add remaining ingredients, select white bread or basic setting and push start. Yield: 1 1/2-pound loaf.

Beer Bread

(Need Bread Machine)

1 pkg. dry yeast
1 c. rye flour
2 1/2 c. bread flour
2 T. wheat germ
1 tsp. salt

1 c. beer, flat, room temp. (leftover
   from last night's bash) ☺
2 T. molasses
2 tsp. orange rind, grated
6 tsp. applesauce, unsweetened
1/4 c. water (120°)

Place all ingredients into bread machine in order given or as directed in your user's manual. Select correct bread cycle and press start.

Quick Beer Bread - Wheat

3 c. packaged biscuit mix (such as Bisquick)
1 c. whole wheat flour
2 T. sugar

2 eggs
1 (12 oz.) can (1 1/2 c.) beer, room temp. ☺

In a mixer bowl, combine the biscuit mix, flour and sugar. Add eggs and beer. Beat with electric mixer about 1 minute, or until well blended. Turn into a greased 5x9x3-inch loaf pan, spreading evenly. Bake in a 350° oven for 50 to 60 minutes, or until done. Cool in pan 10 minutes. Remove and cool on wire rack. Yield: 1 loaf.

Beer Bread

3/4 c. beer (dark or light) ☺
2 T. butter
1 (13 3/4 oz.) pkg. hot roll mix

1 egg
2 T. sugar
1/2 c. wheat germ

In saucepan, heat beer and butter until just warm. Pour into mixer bowl, add yeast from roll mix and dissolve. Add egg, sugar, wheat germ and dry ingredients from roll mix. Mix well. Place in greased bowl, turn once to grease surface. Cover and let rise until double in size (45 to 60 minutes). Punch down, knead and shape into loaf. Place in greased loaf pan and let rise again (30 to 35 minutes). Bake in 350° oven for 40 to 45 minutes.

Rye Beer Bread

2 pkg. dry yeast	**1 T. salt**
1/2 c. warm water	**1 T. caraway seeds**
2 1/2 c. beer ☺	**5 c. rye flour**
1/2 c. shortening	**4 c. white, all-purpose flour**
1 c. dark molasses	**1 egg**

Sprinkle dry yeast in warm water. Stir until dissolved. Heat beer until it just starts to bubble. Remove from heat and add shortening. Add molasses, salt and caraway seeds to beer and stir. Cool until lukewarm and stir in dissolved yeast. Beat in rye flour. Beat in white flour until dough is too firm to beat. Turn out dough onto floured board. Knead until smooth and elastic, 6 to 10 minutes. Put into greased bowl and butter top of dough. Cover and let rise until double, about 1 1/2 hours.

On a lightly-floured board, knead again until smooth. Shape into 2 long loaves or 3 round loaves. Slash top with very sharp knife several times. Brush with egg that has been beaten with 1 tablespoon water. Let loaves stand until doubled in bulk. Brush again with beaten egg. Bake in preheated 350° oven for 40 to 45 minutes.

This is great with sliced turkey or roast beef for a party!

Round Rye with Dark Beer

2 rounds loaves or 3 regular loaves

Great on its own or stuff with spinach dip for an appetizer!

1 1/2 T. active dry yeast	**1 T. salt**
1/2 c. warm water	**3 c. rye flour**
2 c. dark flat beer, room temp. ☺	**2 1/2 to 3 c. white flour, preferably**
2 T. molasses	**unbleached**
2 T. vegetable fat, melted	**Cornmeal**
2 T. crushed caraway seeds	

In a large bowl, dissolve the yeast in the warm water. Stir in the beer, molasses, caraway seeds, salt, rye flour and enough white flour until the dough becomes difficult to stir. Turn the dough out onto a floured working surface and let rest while you clean out and grease your bowl. Knead the dough, adding more white flour as necessary; it will be very tacky, but up to 3 cups white flour in all and about 8 to 10 minutes of kneading should be enough. Return the dough to the greased bowl, cover with plastic wrap and let rise until double in volume, about 2 hours.

Turn the dough out, punch it down, and form into 2 rounds. Place far apart on a greased baking sheet sprinkled with cornmeal. Let rise, covered with a towel, until double, about 45 minutes. Bake the loaves at 375° for 20 to 30 minutes. Cool on racks.

Low-Fat Beer Bread

Yeah, right! Well, we're saving a few calories with lite beer.

3 c. self-rising flour
1/4 c. sugar
1 can lite beer ☺

1 egg, beaten
1 T. water
Melted butter

Mix flour and sugar in bowl. Add beer, watch it foam and mix just until blended. Pour into buttered loaf pan, preferably glass. Combine egg with mixer and brush top of loaf. Let rise 10 minutes. Bake at 350° for 40 to 45 minutes. Brush top with butter while hot.

Great for last minute.

People who drink "light beer" don't like the taste of beer; they just like to pee a lot.
--Captain Brewery, Middleton, WI

Diet Beer Bread

The 1/2-inch slice is about 85 calories. Problem is - I can't eat just one slice. The aroma alone will make you want to dive into it face first!

1 (12 oz.) can light beer ☺
3 T. vegetable oil
1 1/2 c. whole wheat flour
3 T. sugar

1/2 c. water
4 1/2 to 5 c. all-purpose flour
2 pkg. dry yeast
1 1/2 tsp. salt

Combine beer, water and oil in a saucepan; heat to 120° to 130°. Combine 1 1/2 cups all-purpose flour, whole wheat flour, yeast, sugar and salt in a large mixing bowl; add beer mixture. Beat 5 minutes at medium speed. Stir in enough remaining flour to make a soft dough. Turn dough out onto a lightly-floured surface. Knead 8 to 10 minutes. Place dough in a cooking spray-coated bowl, turning to grease the top. Cover; let rise in a warm place until double. Punch down. Divide into half. Shape in loaves. Place into 2 (5x9x3-inch) loaf pans coated with cooking spray. Cover; let rise 45 minutes. Bake at 375° for 30 to 35 minutes.

Rock n' Rolls

3 c. Bisquick
1 can beer ☺

3 T. sugar

Dough will be consistency of cake batter. Put in greased muffin tins or use cupcake foils. Bake at 400° (preheat oven).

B-Studly Muffins

Very good!

2 T. unsalted butter	1/2 tsp. cayenne pepper
1 1/4 c. cornmeal	1 sm. onion, minced
3/4 c. flour	1 egg
2 T. sugar	1 c. beer ☺
1 T. baking powder	1 1/2 c. grated Cheddar cheese

Melt butter and set aside. In large mixing bowl, add flour, cornmeal, sugar, baking powder and cayenne pepper. Add beer and egg to melted butter; mix. Make a well in the center of the dry ingredients and pour in butter mixture. Stir briskly to combine being careful not to overstir. (Batter should be lumpy.) Stir in cheese. Fill muffin cups 2/3-full. Bake at 400° for 20 to 25 minutes. Remove immediately and cool on wire rack.

I know I'm getting better at golf because I'm hitting fewer spectators.
--Gerald Ford

"Corny" Beer Bread

This recipe uses cornmeal and flour.

2 1/2 c. self-rising cornmeal
2 1/2 c. unsifted self-rising flour
5 T. sugar

1 1/2 c. sour cream
1 (12 oz.) can beer ☺
Melted butter, for tops

Use half self-rising flour and half self-rising cornmeal.

Preheat oven to 375°. In large bowl, combine flour and sugar. Add sour cream and beer alternately; mix well. Pour into well-greased (Pam) baking dishes as follows: 2-quart round dish and bake 45 minutes. Brush top with butter, bake 15 to 20 minutes longer (use cake tester in center). Or 4 (16-ounce) round dishes and bake 35 minutes. Brush top with butter, bake 3 to 6 minutes longer (cake tester).

Desserts

FAVORITE RECIPES
FROM MY COOKBOOK

Recipe Name	Page Number

Desserts

Apple Turnovers

Can also use peach, apricot or fig marmalade for filling.

1 lb. all-purpose flour
1/2 tsp. salt
1/2 lb. shortening
1/2 (12 oz.) can beer ☺

Pineapple, peach, fig, apricot or
apple marmalade for filling
Sugar & cinnamon

Sift flour with salt into bowl. Cut shortening into flour with pastry blender or fork until pieces are about the size of large peas. Add beer gradually. Toss with a fork to make a stiff dough. Form into a ball and knead thoroughly until smooth on a lightly-floured board. Roll out dough 1/8-inch thick and cut into 4- or 5-inch circles or 3-inch for mini turnovers. Spoon filling on one side of each circle. Fold over and press edges together with fork. Bake in a 375° oven for 20 minutes, or until browned. Roll hot turnovers in sugar mixed with a little cinnamon.

Money can't buy you happiness -
but it does bring you a more pleasant form of misery.
--Spike Milligan

"Happy Brownies"
(Nothing Illegal!)

24 to 36 servings

These are great brownies. You won't taste the beer!

1 c. all-purpose flour
3/4 c. unsweetened cocoa powder
1/4 tsp. salt
6 T. unsalted room-temp. butter,
  cut into cubes
8 oz. dark bitter-sweet chocolate,
  chopped

3/4 c. white chocolate chips
4 lg. eggs, room temp.
1 c. superfine or granulated sugar
1 1/4 c. Stout beer, room temp. ☺
1 c. semi-sweet chocolate chips
1/4 c. confectioners' sugar, for
  dusting

Preheat oven to 375°. Line a 9x13-inch baking pan with nonstick foil. In a medium bowl, whisk together flour, cocoa powder and salt until evenly combined. Set aside. Melt butter, bitter-sweet chocolate and white chocolate chips in a double boiler over very low heat, stirring constantly, until melted. Remove from heat.

In a large mixing bowl, beat eggs and sugar on high speed until light and fluffy, about 3 minutes. Add melted chocolate mixture, beating until combined. Beat reserved flour mixture into melted chocolate mixture. Whisk in stout beer. The batter will seem a bit thin. Drop semi-sweet chocolate chips evenly on top of batter (some will sink in). Pour into prepared baking pan. Bake 25 to 30 minutes on center rack in oven, until a toothpick inserted in the center comes out almost clean. Let brownies cool, uncovered, to room temperature. Dust with confectioners' sugar before serving.

If beer is cold, put bottle in hot water to help bring it to room temperature.

"Irish Whiskey Frilly Fruit Fry"

6 servings

Now, I want you to have a few beers or drinks of your choice and say this recipe name 10 times without making a mistake. Betcha you can't do it!

2 c. peeled diced apples, pears, peaches or plums, or a mixture of these
4 T. Irish whiskey ☺
2 egg yolks
2/3 c. flat beer ☺
1 T. butter, melted

1 c. all-purpose flour
1/4 tsp. salt
1 T. sugar
2 egg whites
Oil, for deep frying
Confectioners' sugar

Combine diced fruit and whiskey; mix well. Let stand while preparing batter. Beat egg yolks, beer and butter together. Add dry ingredients; beat until no lumps remain. Cover; refrigerate 2 hours. Drain fruit well; mix with batter. Whip egg whites until stiff but not dry. Fold into fritter batter lightly but thoroughly.

Meanwhile, heat 3 inches of oil in deep fryer to 375°. Drop batter by tablespoons into hot oil; cook until golden (3 to 4 minutes). Drain on paper towels. Dust with confectioners' sugar. Serve immediately.

Coffeecake with Yummy Rum Butter Frosting

12 servings

You need a bundt pan. If you make it a day ahead of when you want to serve it, the flavor intensifies.

3 c. all-purpose flour
2 tsp. baking soda
1 tsp. cinnamon
1/2 tsp. allspice
1/2 tsp. cloves
2 c. chopped dates

1 c. chopped walnuts
1 c. butter, softened
2 c. packed dark brown sugar
2 c. beer ☺
2 eggs

Mix dry ingredients; set aside. Combine dates and nuts, stir in small amount of flour mixture and set aside. In large bowl, cream butter and sugar. Add eggs, one at a time. Beat well after each addition, alternating flour mixture with beer. Stir in dates and nuts. Pour into well-greased and floured bundt pan. Bake in 350° oven for 1 hour and 15 minutes, or until tests done. Cool 10 minutes on rack and then turn out to cool. Wrap cake in foil 24 hours before serving. Sprinkle with confectioners' sugar and serve Rum Butter Frosting on side.

Continued on following page.

Continued from preceding page.

FROSTING:
1/2 c. soft butter   **Confectioners' sugar, as needed**
2 T. rum ☺

Whip butter and rum until fluffy. Serve as is or add confectioners' sugar for thicker consistency.

Gingerbread Cake

1 pkg. gingerbread mix   **1/4 c. salad oil**
1/4 tsp. baking soda   **1/2 c. chopped walnuts**
1 1/4 c. beer, room temp. ☺   **20 oz. apple pie filling**

Preheat oven to 350°. Grease sides of a 9-inch pan. Prepare mix using beer instead of water and adding baking soda and oil. Stir in walnuts. Spread apple filling over bottom of pan. Pour batter over apples and bake for 30 to 40 minutes. Use whipped cream as topping.

Sauerkraut and Beer Fudge Cake

I know, you are thinking "Oh gag me!" If you rinse the sauerkraut a few times, you don't taste the sauerkraut or the beer. It provides texture just like carrot cake. I've tried several renditions of this recipe, but the Lutheran's have perfected it!

2/3 c. butter	1 tsp. baking soda
1 1/2 c. sugar	1 tsp. baking powder
3 eggs	1/4 tsp. salt
1 tsp. vanilla	1 c. beer ☺
1/2 c. cocoa	2/3 c. sauerkraut, rinsed, drained
2 1/2 c. unsifted flour	& chopped

Cream butter and sugar until light and fluffy. Beat in eggs and vanilla. Sift together cocoa, flour, baking soda, baking powder and salt. Add dry ingredients to the creamed mixture alternately with beer, starting and ending with the dry ingredients. Stir in the chopped sauerkraut (I rinse the sauerkraut with water a few times, don't squeeze all the moisture out). Pour into a greased and floured bundt pan or 2 (9-inch) pans. Bake at 325° to 350° for about 50 minutes. Cool.

Continued on following page.

Continued from preceding page.

CHOCOLATE CREAM CHEESE FROSTING:

8 oz. semi-sweet chocolate	2 c. sifted confectioners' sugar
6 oz. cream cheese, softened	1/4 tsp. salt
2 T. light cream	1 tsp. vanilla

Melt chocolate in top of double boiler over hot water, not boiling water. Cool slightly and blend in the cream cheese and cream. Slowly add sugar, mixing well. Stir in the salt and vanilla. Frost cooled cake.

The cardiologist's diet: If it tastes good, spit it out.
--Anonymous

"Divot" Chocolate Beer Cake

If you can't stomach the thought of sauerkraut in your cake, try this one.

2/3 c. butter, room temp.	2 1/2 c. all-purpose flour
2 c. sugar	1 1/2 tsp. baking soda
2 eggs, beaten	1/2 tsp. salt
2 sq. (2 oz.) unsweetened	3/4 c. buttermilk
chocolate, melted	1/2 c. beer ☺

FROSTING:

1/2 c. whipping cream	2 sq. (2 oz.) unsweetened
1 c. sugar	chocolate, melted
	2 T. butter

   Cream butter and sugar. Add eggs and beat until light. Blend in the chocolate. Sift flour, baking soda and salt together. Add to creamed mixture along with the buttermilk. Blend until smooth. Stir in the beer and beat until light. Butter and flour 2 (9-inch) round cake pans. Turn batter into pans. Smooth top. Bake at 350° for 35 to 40 minutes, or until cakes test done. Remove from pans. Cool on wire racks.

   While cakes bake, make the frosting. Bring 1/2 cup of the cream and the sugar to a boil in a heavy saucepan. Boil 2 minutes. Add the chocolate and simmer for 5 minutes. Beat in the butter. Spread half of the filling mixture on each of the cake rounds as you stack them. Sides of the cake may be left unfrosted, if desired. Cut into wedges to serve.

"Cabana Boy" Beer Cake

This is good!

1/2 c. butter	1/2 c. walnuts, chopped
2 c. sugar	1/4 tsp. salt
4 eggs	1 tsp. baking soda
1/2 c. orange juice	1 tsp. nutmeg
1/2 c. apple butter (store-bought or homemade)	1 tsp. cloves
	1 tsp. cinnamon
3/4 c. honey	1 tsp. allspice
4 c. sifted all-purpose flour	1 c. beer ☺
2 tsp. baking powder	1 c. raisins

Preheat oven to 325°. Cream butter and sugar until fluffy. Add eggs, one at a time, beating well after each addition. Add orange juice, apple butter and honey. Mix well. Add sifted dry ingredients alternately with beer, beginning and ending with dry ingredients. Add raisins and nuts which have been coated with flour. Pour batter in greased and floured tube pan. Bake at 325° for 1 hour and 20 minutes. Sprinkle top and sides with confectioners' sugar.

An intelligent man is sometimes forced to be drunk to spend time with his friends.
--Ernest Hemingway

"Field of Dreams" Moist Beer Cake with Lemon Frosting

Make 1 to 2 days before planning to serve.

1 c. butter	1 tsp. cinnamon
1 c. brown sugar	1/2 tsp. allspice
2 eggs, beaten	1/2 tsp. cloves
3 c. flour	1 1/4 c. walnuts or pecans
1/2 tsp. salt	2 c. dates
2 tsp. baking soda	2 c. beer (1 pt.) ☺

Cream butter; add sugar and cream. Add beaten eggs and beat well. Beat flour and spices into mixture (reserve 3 tablespoons). Slowly add beer and blend. Toss nuts and fruit with flour; fold in. Pour into greased and floured 10-inch tube pan. Bake at 350° for 60 to 75 minutes. Cool 10 minutes and then turn out. Cover and refrigerate overnight.

Do not serve same day. Wrap in foil and can keep in refrigerator for 10 days to 2 weeks.

LEMON GLAZE:
1 1/2 c. confectioners' sugar, sifted   3 to 4 T. lemon juice

Blend until smooth and serve on cake.

Mama's Molasses Beer Cake

1 c. molasses	1/4 tsp. baking soda
1/2 c. butter	1/2 tsp. cinnamon
1 can beer ☺	1/2 tsp. nutmeg
1 1/4 c. raisins	1/2 tsp. ginger
2 2/3 c. sifted flour	1 1/4 c. coarsely-chopped pecans
1/2 tsp. baking powder	

Combine molasses, butter and beer in a saucepan and heat until the butter melts. Stir in raisins and let the mixture cool 15 minutes. Sift together dry ingredients. Stir in the nuts. When the beer mixture is cool, pour it over dry ingredients and stir until smooth. Pour batter into greased and floured rectangular pan. Bake at 350° for 1 hour.

GLAZE:

1 c. 10X sugar	Liquid honey, to moisten

Pour over cake.

A blond got really excited...
finished jigsaw puzzle in 6 months...box said "2-4 years!"
--Anonymous

"Bo-dacious" Beer Cake

Add frosting of your choice.

1/2 c. butter	2 1/2 c. sifted all-purpose flour
1 1/2 c. sugar	1/4 tsp. salt
3 egg yolks	1 c. beer (your choice) ☺
1 tsp. vanilla	1/2 tsp. baking powder
3 egg whites	1/8 tsp. cream of tartar

Preheat oven to 375°. Cream soft butter and sugar until fluffy. Add egg yolks, one at a time, beating well after each. Blend in sifted dry ingredients alternately with beer, beginning and ending with dry ingredients. Add vanilla. Sprinkle in baking powder. Beat egg whites and cream of tartar until stiff. Fold gently but thoroughly into batter. Grease and flour two 9-inch layer pans. Pour batter into pans. Bake at 375° for 25 minutes, or until cake tests done.

Cherry Beer Cake

This is really moist and tastes great!

2/3 c. butter
2 eggs
2 1/4 c. flour
1 c. beer ☺
1 (8 oz.) btl. maraschino cherries
1/4 c. cherry juice

2 c. sugar
2 sq. unsweetened chocolate, melted
2 tsp. baking soda
3/4 c. buttermilk
1/2 c. nuts, chopped

FROSTING:
8 oz. cream cheese, softened
1 stick butter, softened

1 lb. powdered sugar
2 tsp. vanilla

Cream shortening and sugar. Add eggs and melted chocolate, mixing well. Sift flour and baking soda; add to creamed mixture alternately with beer and buttermilk. Cut cherries and add to creamed mixture along with cherry juice and nuts. Blend well. Pour into 9x13-inch pan and bake at 350° for about 40 minutes.

Blend ingredients together for frosting. Wait for cake to cool and then spread frosting on top.

Beer Fruit Cake

1 c. beer ☺
2 c. raisins
1 c. packed brown sugar
1/3 c. butter
1 tsp. cinnamon
1 tsp. allspice
1 tsp. salt
1/2 tsp. nutmeg

2 c. cake flour (this can be found at your grocery near all-purpose flour)
1 tsp. double-acting baking powder
1 tsp. baking soda
1 1/4 c. chopped nuts
1 c. chopped dried fruits or apples

Heat oven to 325°. Boil first 8 ingredients together for 3 minutes. Allow to cool. Sift cake flour before measuring; resift with baking powder and baking soda. Stir flour mixture gradually into other mixture. Add chopped nuts and fruit. Bake in greased tube pan for 1 hour. When cool, sprinkle with powdered sugar and add Citrus Glaze.

CITRUS GLAZE:
1 1/4 c. confectioners' sugar
1/4 c. lemon, orange or lime juice

1 tsp. vanilla extract

Mix above ingredients until smooth. Drizzle over cake.

Beer Dump Cake

1 bundt cake

This is fast and easy. You won't taste the beer. You can add store-bought frosting if you like.

1 pkg. yellow cake mix   **1/4 c. oil**
1 pkg. vanilla instant pudding   **4 eggs**
1 c. beer (do not use flat beer) ☺

Mix cake mix and pudding in a large bowl. Add beer and oil. Mix slightly. Add eggs. Beat until creamy. Pour into bundt pan. Bake at 350° for 55 minutes. Cool and remove from pan.

Friends don't let friends drink Light Beer.
--Anonymous

Devils Food Dump Cake

1 pkg. devils food cake mix	2 eggs
1 1/3 c. beer ☺	1/4 tsp. baking soda
1/2 c. oil	

Add ingredients and follow cake mix instructions, then cool and cover with frosting.

CHOCOLATE FROSTING:

1/4 c. unsweetened cocoa	1/4 c. milk
1 c. granulated sugar (not	1 tsp. vanilla
powdered)	4 T. butter (not margarine)

Mix all ingredients and melt over medium heat slowly. Let boil exactly 1 minute. Beat immediately until it begins to thicken. Pour quickly onto cake and spread evenly.

Beer Cheese Cake

One 8-inch cake

You need a springform pan for this recipe.

1 lb. cream cheese, softened	**1/4 c. unsalted butter, melted &**
1/2 c. sugar	**cooled**
2 T. flour	**Finely-grated rind of 1 lemon**
4 eggs	**1 c. lager beer ☺**
	1/2 c. mixed currants & raisins

In an electric mixer, beat the cheese for a minute. Add the sugar and beat until blended. Beat in the flour and eggs, one by one, then add the remaining ingredients in the order given. Pour into a greased 8-inch diameter, 3-inch deep springform pan and bake on the middle level of a preheated 350° oven for 1 1/2 hours. Remove to a cake rack to cool.

No-Joke Crock-Pot Beer Cake

2/3 c. butter
1 1/2 c. brown sugar
3 eggs
2 1/2 c. flour
1 1/2 tsp. baking powder
1/4 tsp. baking soda

1 tsp. cinnamon
1/4 tsp. nutmeg
1 1/2 c. beer ☺
1 1/4 c. chopped walnuts
1 1/4 c. raisins

Cream butter and sugar until light and fluffy. Add eggs, one at a time, and mix well. Add flour, baking soda, baking powder, cinnamon and nutmeg to creamy mixture alternately with beer. Stir in walnuts and raisins. Pour mixture into well-buttered and floured cake pan that will fit into crock-pot. Cover tin with 4 or 5 paper towels. Put into pot. Put lid on crock-pot loosely to allow steam to escape. Cook on high for 3 1/2 hours, or until cake is done. Remove pan from pot and allow cake to cool on wire rack for 15 minutes before removing from pan.

We're not here for a long time, but we are here for a <u>Good Time</u>!
--Anonymous

INDEX

BEER BOMBS

Dogs Bollocks..1
The Canadian Gulp 1
Ball Hooter...1
Sip and Get Funky...2
Outhouse Slammer..2
The Extinguisher..2
Michelada 3
Vermo 3
Good 'n Plenty 3
Green Goblin 4
Hot 'n' Frosty 4
Naval Destroyer...4
Lunch Box...5
Miner's Lung..5
Red Eye 5
Faith, Hope and Garrity 6
Boilermaker 6
Deer Hunter 7
Spudgun..7
Power Drill 8
Brian's Juice 8
Black and Tan 8
Heavy Navel 9
Flaming Dr. Pepper 9
Backfire on the Freeway 9
Baha Fog 10
Bite Me 10
Beeraquirilla 10
AJ's Bubbling Brew 11
Celtic War Party...11
Bud Bomb Breakfast..12
Beer Buster..12

STARTING LINE UP
(Appetizers)

Caramelized Garlic Breath 13
Chilly Cheese Dip..14
Cheezy-Weezy Beer Dip 15
"Bubba's" Beer Batter 16
Con Queso Dip 17
Beer-Boiled Shrimp 17
Beer-Battered Veggies 18
Welsch Rabbit with Beer...19
Fried Zucchini in Beer Batter 20
Wing 'a Ding 'n Drummies 21
Cheese n' Beer Fondue 22
Spicy Fondue...23
Easy Kielbasa Fondue...24
Buffalo Wings for a Party 25
"Bull Fightin" Black Bean and Beef Chili Dip 26-27
"Macho Nachos".. 28-29
"Buckin" Barbecue Cocktail Sausage 30
Easy Beer, Cheese and Veggie Dip 30
Sissy-Chicken Salad Puffy Shells 31
"Fluffer Nutter" Sandwich..32

SOUPS, STEWS, SALADS & SIDE DISHES

SOUPS & STEWS

Beer Stew 33
Belgian Beef Stew 34
Beef and Beer Stew..35
Irish Stew 36
Stewed Beef and Bread 37
Easy and Quick Beef Stew..38
Seafood Chowder 39
Broccoli Cheese Soup 40
Beer and Cheese Soup...41
Potato Beer Soup...42
Mushroom and Beer Soup 43

Sweet Potato Soup 44-45
When You're Broke Beer Soup 46
Garlic Beer Soup 47

SALADS & SIDE DISHES

Seafood Salad 48
Cranberry Salad 48
Greeny Beany Potato Salad 49
Pasta Salad 50
Beer and Spud Salad 51
Eggplant Pasta in Beer 52
Hot German Potato Salad 53
Chicken Pasta Salad 54
Stuffed Fried Squash 55-56
Southern Cooked Greens in Beer 57
Kickin' Beans 58
Fried Asparagus 59
Carbo Beer Batter Baked Potatoes 60
Warm Potato Salad 61
Red Cabbage 62
Marinara Sauce with Beer 63
Sauerkraut Stuffing 64-65

MARINADES & SAUCES

MARINADES

Beefy Steak Marinade 67
Simple Steak Marinade 68
Marinade for Pork Chops 68
"Plumber-Butt" Marinade for Beef, Pork or Chicken 69
Beef Marinade 69
Chicky-Chick Marinade 70
Grass-Skirt Marinade 71
Simple Chicken Marinade 71
Horseradish Beef Marinade 72

SAUCES

Beef Slop 73
A "Boat"-Load of Sauce...74
Sa-weet Bar-B-Q Marinade and Sauce.....................................75
"Sock-It-To-Ya" Barbecue Sauce 76
"Road Kill" Bar-B-Q Sauce...77
Strumin' and Drumin' Bar-B-Q Sauce 78
SSSSS-Spicy Citrus Barbie-Q Sauce 79
Chicken Lickin' Barbie-Q Sauce 79
Ba, Ba, Baran... Beer Batter 80
Seafood Marinade..81

FISH

Coconut Beer Shrimp To Die For...83
"Sand Trapped" Deep-Fried Shrimp 84
"Royal Flush" Hot Bar-B-Qued Shrimp 85
Fried Shrimp Marinade 86
Shrimp 'N Beer Batter..86
Beer Broiled Shrimp 87
Fried Fish in Beer Batter 87
Light and Fluffy Beer Batter..88
"Great Catch" Beer Batter Trout 88
Fish Beer Batter..89
"Bait and Tackle" Seafood Kabobs...90
Shrimp and Scallops with Pecan Rice 91
"Lured" Grilled Tuna..92
Grilled Halibut or Fish Fillets 93
Grilled Fish...93
Baked Cod with Almonds..94
Fried Scrod with Spicy Fruit Sauce 95-96
Grilled Fiesta Fish Tuna with Salsa...97
Fried Soft-Shell Crabs 98

POULTRY

"My Other Brother" Daryl's Chicken..99
"Hammered" Fried Chicken...100
"Cluckin Hooters"...101
Drunk Chicken..102
Beer Batter Chicken..103
Barbeque Turkey Drumsticks 104
"Prize Fightin" Beer Batter Chicken with Onions 105
Goose Your Chicken..106
"Birdied" Chicken Pot Pie.. 107-108
"No. 2 Handicap" Chicken 'n' Rice 109
You Callin' Me Chicken? 110
Chicken Baked Chicken.. 111
"High Fly" Chicken Chili 112
Billy Bob's Bar-B-Q Chicken 112

BEEF, VEAL, LAMB & GAME

BEEF

"Blitzed" Marinated Steak 113
Coffee Encrusted Steaks 114
"Touch Down" Steak..115
Marinated Steak...115
Bag It Bar-B-Qued Steak 116
Beef Tenderloin and Mushroom Gravy...117
Barbecue Brisket 117
"How About That" Beef, Beer, Wine and Sherry................................118
"7th Inning Stretch" Slow-Cooked Pot Roast with Dried Fruit..........119
Braised London Broil 120-121
Easy Beef 'n Beer...121
Beef 'n Brewsky 122
German Pot Roast...123
Beef, Brew and Cabbage...124
Italian Stallion Beef...125
"Punt It" Pot Roast 126
Two-Fisted Stroganoff Steak Sandwiches 127
Napoleon-Style Ribs..128

1st and Goal Short Ribs with a Kick 129
"1st and 10" Shisk K-Bobs...130
Beef 'n Brew Kabobs 131
Lacrosse Onion Burgers...132
Rugby Bar-B-Qued Beef...132
"Prize-Fightin" Bar-B-Que Meat Balls...133
Beer and Bacon Spaghetti Sauce...134
"Par for the Course" Shredded Beef...135
"Knock Out" Chili Con Carne...136
"World Series" Chili for Dogs...137
"Double Play" Beer Chili..138
"Lineman" Beef Goulash..139

VEAL
Stuffed Veal..140

LAMB
Leg of Lamb..141
Lamb with Sour Cream and Capers 142

GAME
Venison Stir-Fry 143
Braised Rabbit or Chicken in Beer 144

PORK
"Atlanta-Style Ribs"...145
This Little Piggy Went to Market Stew...146
Quick and Easy Pork Stew with Fruit 147
"Three Pointer" Grilled Pork Roast 148
Honey Grilled Pork 149
Brainless Ham on the Grill..150
Marinated Brats 151
"Full House" Brats 'n Buns..152
Polish Sausage with Cabbage and Apples..153
Brats 'n Sauce 154
Ribs and Beer 155
Bon Bon's Babyback Ribs 156
"Giddy-Up 409" Ribs..157

Chinese-Style Ribs..158
Confused Grill..159
Happy Honey Garlic Ribs 160
Sloppy Barb-Q Ribs...161
Ribs for 2...161
Rag Apple Ribs 162
"He-Man" Country-Style Ribs.. 163-164
Slathered Mesquite-Smoked Ribs 165-166
"Go Golfin" Beer BBQ Ribs...167
Teriyaki Pork Chops..168
"Shoot Some Hoops" Bar-B-Cued Pork Chops.................................169

BREADS

"Morning After Breakfast" Bourbon, Beer
    and Sweet Potato Waffles 171
"Batter Up" Buttermilk Beer Pancakes...172
Catcher's Favorite Beer Batter Pancakes......................................172
Sweet Beer Bread with Raisins 173
Corn Fritters in Beer Batter 173
Stud Muffins...174
Hungry Man Beer Biscuits 174
Beer Cheese Bread 175
Beer Bread...175
Quick Beer Bread - Wheat 176
Beer Bread...176
Rye Beer Bread 177
Round Rye with Dark Beer 178
Low-Fat Beer Bread 179
Diet Beer Bread 180
Rock 'n Rolls...180
B-Studly Muffins 181
"Corny" Beer Bread...182

DESSERTS

Apple Turnovers...183
"Happy Brownies"..184
"Irish Whiskey Frilly Fruit Fry"...185
Coffeecake with Yummy Rum Butter Frosting............................186-187
Sauerkraut and Beer Fudge Cake...188-189
"Divot" Chocolate Beer Cake...190
"Cabana Boy" Beer Cake..191
"Field of Dreams" Moist Beer Cake with Lemon Frosting.................192
Mama's Molasses Beer Cake..193
"Bp-Dacious" Beer Cake...194
Cherry Beer Cake...195
Beer Fruit Cake..196
Beer Dump Cake..197
Deviuls Food Dump Cake...198
Beer Cheese Cake...199
No-Joke Crock-Pot Beer Cake...200

Converting to Metric Measurements

MEASURES:

English	Metric
1/4 tsp.	1 ml
1/2 tsp.	2 ml
1 tsp.	5 ml
1 tbsp.	15 ml
2 tbsp.	25 ml
1/4 cup	50 ml
1/3 cup	75 ml
1/2 cup	125 ml
2/3 cup	150 ml
3/4 cup	175 ml
1 cup	250 ml
1 1/2 cups	375 ml
2 cups	500 ml

WEIGHTS

For fish, meat, poultry and bulk fruits and vegetables

English	Metric
1 lb.	500 g
3/4 lb. or 12 oz.	375 g
1/2 lb. or 8 oz.	250 g
1/4 lb. or 4 oz.	125 g

OVEN TEMPERATURES

Fahrenheit	Celsius
300°	150°
325°	160°
350°	180°
375°	190°
400°	200°
425°	220°
450°	230°

DEEP-FAT FRYING TEMPERATURES

Fahrenheit	Celsius
350°	170°
375°	190°
385°	195°
395°	200°

CANDY-MAKING TEMPERATURES

Stage	Celsius (Fahrenheit)
Thread Stage	110°-112° C. (230°-234° F.)
Soft-Ball Stage	112°-115° C. (234°-240° F.)
Firm-Ball Stage	118°-120° C. (244°-248° F.)
Hard-Ball Stage	121°-130° C. (250°-266° F.)
Soft-Crack Stage	132°-143° C. (270°-290° F.)
Hard-Crack Stage	149°-154° C. (300°-310° F.)

PAN SIZES

Inches	Centi-meters	Capacity (Liters)
Rectangular		
10 x 6 x 1 1/2	25 x 15 x 4	1.5
11 x 7 x 1 1/2	28 x 18 x 4	1.8
12 x 7 1/2 x 2	30 x 19 x 5	2.5
13 x 9 x 2	33 x 23 x 5	3.5
Square		
8 x 8 x 2	20 x 20 x 5	1.8
9 x 9 x 2	23 x 23 x 5	2.4
Round		
8 x 1 1/2	20 x 4	1.2
9 x 1 1/2	23 x 4	1.5
Tube		
9-inch	23 x 9	2.7
10-inch	25 x 10	3.1
Jelly Roll		
15 x 10 x 1	39 x 27 x 25	
Loaf		
8 x 4 x 2	22 x 11 x 6	1.5
9 x 5 x 3	23 x 13 x 8	2.0
Pie Pans		
4 1/4-inch	11 x 3	
9-inch	23 x 3	
10-inch	25 x 4	

210